# BILINGUAL EDUCATION

SUNY Series, Teacher Empowerment and School Reform
Edited by Henry A. Giroux and Peter L. McLaren

# BILINGUAL EDUCATION

*A Dialogue with the Bakhtin Circle*

Marcia Moraes

STATE UNIVERSITY OF NEW YORK PRESS

Published by
State University of New York Press, Albany

For information, address State University of New York Press,
State University Plaza, Albany, N.Y., 12246

Production by Cathleen Collins
Marketing by Theresa Abad Swierzowski

**Library of Congress Cataloging in Publication Data**

Moraes, Marcia, 1960–
    Bilingual education : a dialogue with the Bakhtin circle / Marcia
Moraes.
        p.      cm. — (SUNY series, teacher empowerment and school
reform)
    Includes bibliographical references and index.
    ISBN 0–7914–3021–9 (hc : alk. paper). — ISBN 0–7914–3022–7 (pb :
alk. paper)
    1. Education, Bilingual—Philosophy.  2. Critical pedagogy.
3. Bakhtin, M. M. (Mikhail Mikhaĭlovich), 1895–1975.  4. Voloshinov,
V. N.  I. Title.  II. Series: Teacher empowerment and school
reform.
LC3715.M67  1996
371.97—dc20                                                    95–41252
                                                                       CIP

10  9  8  7  6  5  4  3  2  1

*To my beloved parents, Wilson and Maria Izabel*
*—for their endless comprehension and love*


*To Peter McLaren*
*—with whom I learned that world is possibility*

# CONTENTS

# FOREWORD

To say the spirit of democracy continues to be betrayed across nearly all sectors of U.S. politics sounds, ironically enough, too optimistic for these "new" times. In order to be betrayed, the spirit of democracy has to still be alive and, to a certain extent, still kicking. A strong case could be made against this claim.

Recent attacks on affirmative action, multiculturalism, and bilingual education have created a theater of cynicism so charged that it is threatening to erupt against citizens in all walks of life, but in particular, against non-English-speaking students in our schools. Perhaps nowhere is this eruption more threatening than in the area of bilingual education.

Strutting across the political stage like self-righteous demogogues, fueling anti-immigrant sentiment, and playing on the fear, anger, and paranoia of Euro-Americans, politicians are mustering an assault against human dignity and social justice in the name of freedom and democracy. As Senate Majority Leader Bob Dole calls for the end of most bilingual programs throughout the country, his boneless face uncoiling amidst a crowd of his fellow legionnaires, his blue overseas cap with the emblem of Kansas—his home state—emblazoned in gold braid, shielding narrow, cadaverous eyes, and a thin-lipped smile, he is, for all intents and purposes, uttering a full-throated denunciation of the very principles of democracy that elected officials are sworn to defend. The rhetoric is filled with the all-too-familiar xenophobic, us-against-them machosniffery: They are here to divide us; to chip away our unity, and eventually erode our heritage, our harmony, and the ties that bind us together as a nation. They can't be trusted; they speak a strange, foreign language; they are less civilized and, well—less American! Dole's defense of the American way of life echoes the ideological sentiments of fellow presidential hopefuls Pete Wilson, Pat Buchanan, and Phil Gramm in their refusal to understand how their definition of what it means to be "American" is largely antithetical to the spirit of democracy in the eyes of many citizens of the United States.

It is decidedly more difficult to script a counter-offensive to the toxic overdrive of a national campaign fueled by hate, fear, and anger, than it is to denounce bilingual education as anti-American. It is at this historical juncture in which the spectre of the illegal immigrant is stage managed by political functionaries to inspire latent visions of ethnic and racial purity, that the work of Marcia Moraes takes on such urgency and singular importance.

A Brazilian educator whose own second language is English, Moraes offers an important perspective on U.S. bilingual education, including its philosophical, epistemological, and ethical assumptions, as well as its policies and practices. *Bilingual Education: A Dialogue with the Bakhtin Circle* is a work rich in poststructuralist, Marxian, and sociolinguistic insight, a perspective that needs to be read and defended lest U.S. educators succumb to the current ideological hegemony surrounding U.S. education in general and bilingual education in particular.

Working from the premise that a dialogized heteroglossia surrounds each utterance, and that language constitutes an ideological and mutable sign, Moraes offers a powerful defense of bilingual education. In her view, bilingual education needs to move beyond a concern with language acquisition, because language does not just reflect reality, but also refracts reality. In other words, language is always and inevitably part of an ideological and cultural process.

Not only does Moraes link language to the exercise, reproduction, and transformation of power, she is able to reanimate the relationship among the production of knowledge and the physiognomy of identity. Informed largely by the writings of Voloshinov, Bakhtin, and Freire, Moraes uncovers the powerful effect that language has on students' lives and the way in which students understand and interpret each others' worlds. Her work both informs and incites us, providing new ways of political and ethical action that can be exercised by concerned educators. Her analysis of the approach to dialogue undertaken by the Bakhtin circle and Paulo Freire (which differ in fundamental ways, the former emphasizing relationality and interaction, the latter emphasizing critical self-reflexivity) moves beyond a discourse that deals mainly with the architectonics of oppression, and into the terrain of hope and possibility through an articulation of what Moraes calls "a dialogic-critical pedagogy." Bilingual education in this instance is rewritten to mean more than mutual understanding but political praxis.

Moraes is concerned, first and foremost, with the agency of the marginal, with the narrative strategies of the diasporic, with the counter-discourses of the dispossessed who inhabit a "stereophany of languages" (Bhabha, 1994, p. 180). Rehearsing some of the major themes of contemporary politics surrounding language and bilingualism—the ideology of signification; the imperial unconscious and the political consciousness of imperialism; language and identity; the death of the subject; the production of critical agency—Moraes ventures, as Homi Bhabha (1994) would put it, "outside the sentence" and into a bilingual/bicultural world where we encounter the indeterminacy of discourses and discursive strategies capable of contesting the governing ideologies, policies, and social practices surrounding citizenship and identity in the United States.

Furthermore, we are introduced to a discursive realm not of consensus and compromise but rather one of political contestation and ideological struggle in which new structures of temporality, new strategies of comprehension, new epistemological conditions for interpretation, and new forms of ethical address and value-coding are given pedagogical promise.

Moraes invites bilingual education to explore its own limits and disrupt attempts by interest groups comfortably ensconsed ("enfleshed") within the dominant culture to ideologically (con)fuse nationalism with restricting public discourse to the English language and militarizing national borders. From Moraes's critically informed perspective, bilingual education can be seen as both a way of life and a way of resisting social, cultural, and material relations of domination and exploitation. Joining Voloshinov, she reveals that signifiers never float free from the messy web of agonistic and competitive semiotic maneuverings and social meaning-making activities—as the fashionable insurgency of some poststructuralists would suggest. Rather, she argues that signification is inextricably connected to ways of reading and writing the world (as Freire would have it) and always has a continuous yet indeterminate relationship to the subject. The subject, therefore, becomes the aftereffect of the intersubjective exchange (Bhabha, 1994, p. 188). In this view, bilingual education can help resist a narrative closure of identity, preventing a permanent anchoring of signification.

Moraes does not advocate a form of agency (individual or collective) that is based on teleology or ontology but rather invites the construction of a collective praxis that is always in negotiation and attentive to moral and historical contingency. Her analysis brings to mind a view of subjectivity recently articulated by Homi Bhabha (1994) in which the subject is the enunciative subject of heteroglossia and dialogism. In this view, agency is always discursive, it is realized outside of the subject's role as autonomous author; rather, it is revealed through an understanding of the ideological swindle of autonomous, self-directed authorship and through an understanding of how the trick of autonomous authorship is produced, circulated, and consumed. As Bhabha notes, agency is located at the level of the sign, occurring as a temporal break, as the overlapping of sign and symbol and their indeterminate articulation through an enunciative "time lag." It is in the disjunctive present of the utterance that resistance is made possible, that subaltern agency is articulated outside of binaristic relations, and that relocation and reinscription are made possible (Bhabha, 1994, p. 193).

The totalizing and unified chain of discourse that has become forged on the anvil of Western imperialism and hammered into the mail suit of the colonizer can be unlinked by the practices of bilingual education. According to Moraes, bilingual/bicultural education offers a new discursive temporality and a possibility for the creation of hybrid knowledges and new orderings of meanings where the internal difference of Euro-American society is reiterated in terms of, for instance, Latino/a cultures, that is, in terms of the dominant national culture's relation to its "other." In this instance, the generic, negative subject position reserved for the minority "other" within the totalizing myths of the national culture can be politically and pedagogically challenged.

Moraes underscores why bilingual education is so dangerous in these new times: Practiced from a critical-dialogic perspective, it can take us beyond nativist and supremacist ascriptions of national identity to a new form of ethnicity and new types of social identifications that challenge the immutability of the Western citizen of the empire. Here, bilingual education is able to rupture, unsettle, and desacralize the assumptions of Euro-American dominance, introducing new currents of cultural translations, new relations of sociality and new modalities of political agency (McLaren, 1995).

*Bilingual Education: A Dialogue with the Bakhtin Circle* offers the beginning of what we could call a critical bilingualism. That is, a bilingual/bicultural education that is centered around understanding difference as more than simply celebrating diversity. Rather, understanding difference becomes a way of interrogating the social construction of difference as it is constituted within asymmetrical relations of power and in terms of relations of class, sexuality, ethnicity, and gender. In this way it offers a political and pedagogical platform from which minority communities can negotiate their collective identifications and establish a solidarity among ethnicities. It becomes an important social semiotic approach in analyzing how we represent ourselves to others and how others are represented in relation to ourselves.

A critical bilingualism becomes, in this view, the promise of the present and a central hope for the future of democracy. If U.S. politicians, policymakers, and school administrators could listen to the ideas presented by Marcia Moraes in this volume with the same attentiveness they give to national opinion polls, and act upon them in the same spirit of democratic transformation that this book reflects, then perhaps this country could begin to move beyond the "us-against-them" rhetoric that frames the country's current conversation about bilingual education, affirmative action, and multiculturalism and start to heal the deep wounds inflicted on this nation by present policies built upon misunderstanding and fear. Perhaps then we could begin to take an important step in refashioning democracy in relation to much-needed narratives of trust, dignity, and respect.

Peter McLaren
Los Angeles, 1995

# ACKNOWLEDGMENTS

I will take the risk of acknowledging extraordinary people but I know that these words will never express what I really owe them.

My deepest thanks to Peter McLaren whose daily encouragement, scholarly orientation, commitment, and friendship were crucial to make my dreams come true. My special thanks to Jenny McLaren whose friendship was vital in a myriad of moments during this journey. I definitely think words cannot explain how grateful I am to this unique couple of friends.

I profoundly thank Nelda Cambron-McCabe and also Miami University [Ohio] where this project had its beginning. Special thanks to Richard Quantz for contributing significantly in each phase of this work's development. I am equally grateful to Dennis Carlson, Thomas Oldenski, Susan Reilly, Frances Fowler, Joan Wink, Cathleen Collins, and Michele Liberti-Lansing for their immense contributions in revisions of this text.

Huge thanks to my special friends: Sílvia Carvalho, André Loss, Thomas Oldenski, and Khaula Murthada whose patience and friendship are always above any expectation. Finally, I would like to take this brief opportunity to endlessly thank Priscilla Ross, SUNY Press editor, for being someone who gave me fundamental and unforgettable support for this book project.

# INTRODUCTION

The purpose of this book is to analyze bilingual education in relation to the epistemological assumptions of the Bakhtin circle, especially those assumptions addressed by Mikhail Bakhtin and Valentin Voloshinov. The analysis is focused on language as a social entity, from the perspective of Bakhtinian dialogic existence. Briefly, this five-chapter book includes an analysis of the major laws and policies of bilingual education in the United States; the current debate involving English-only versus English-plus; an analysis of the theory addressed by the Bakhtin circle, from the perspective of critical social theory; a discussion of critical/radical pedagogy connected to Paulo Freire's dialogic pedagogy; and the ways in which the theories addressed by the Bakhtin circle can deepen the political and social project of critical/radical pedagogy. Furthermore, the analysis also includes an examination of structuralist linguistic theories such as those advanced by Ferdinand de Saussure and Noam Chomsky. My attempt is to highlight a comparison between structuralist linguistics and the theories addressed by the Bakhtin circle as a means of developing a critical understanding of existing trends within bilingual education research.

I am particularly interested in discussing the Bakhtin circle's work in relation to bilingual education for three primary reasons. First, bilingual education is strongly connected to my cultural background—an individual from Latin America whose second language is English. Bilingual education is also inextricably linked to my professional background, which involves the study of language acquisition, linguistic theory, and learning processes. Second, bilingual education is a crucial field in the United States. At the present time, U.S. teachers are encouraged to teach for diversity; the demographic changes in the United States demand this kind of teaching. Third, Brazilian public schools follow a national curriculum, which declares that students in middle and high school should learn one foreign language (English and/or French). Some public schools offer both English and French programs. Other public schools offer only English programs. Furthermore, in a situation very similar to that of the United States, Brazil is a mixed country whose history reflects a cultural and ethnic polyphony in which generations of native Brazilians, Africans, and European immigrants exist within a multiplicity of voices that were and still are very often overlooked, if not dehumanized.

Jim Cummins (in press a) argues that "the history of the education of culturally diverse students in the United States and most other countries is a history of thinly disguised perpetuation of the coercive relations of power that operate in the wider society." This description is especially appropriate in the current context of Brazil. The Brazilian population embraces a large variety of cultural backgrounds because of its large number of immigrants from many other countries. Yet, because of Brazil's history of slavery (until 1888) and miscegenation, the history of these immigrants as well as nonwhite and Native Brazilians is a history of social invisibility and hidden segregation.[1] These groups were always neglected in curriculum development, especially during the years of civil dictatorship (Getúlio Vargas's government—1937–1945) followed some years later by military dictatorship. The main goal of these two dictatorships was to develop a sense of nationalism and patriotism. However, patriotism and nationalism represented a unified culture and a single national identity. As Carmen Nava (1993) remarks,

> the Vargas government enacted a series of measures designed to restrict the political activities of foreigners and to control immigration from Italy, Germany, and Japan. Newly vigorous state apparatus enabled government to require aliens to register with the police and to deport them for suspicious activity, and new immigration was curtailed. Moreover, immigrants would no longer be allowed to live apart in their own culturally isolated

---

1. For a broader understanding of Brazilian ethnic relations see Martin Marger's (1994) *Race and Ethnic Relations: American and Global Perspectives.* See also Howard Winant's (1992) "The Other Side of the Process: Racial Formation in Contemporary Brazil," in George Yúdice, Jean Franco, and Juan Flores (eds.) *On Edge: The Crisis of Contemporary Latin American Culture.*

colonies. Foreign language newspapers were prohibited, and foreign place names were changed into Portuguese. All schools were required to have Brazilian principals, all instruction was to be in Portuguese, and parents could no longer send their children abroad to school. (p. 11)

However, it was during the military dictatorship (1964–1985) that Brazil experienced a major attempt at unifying the educational arena compatible with its military goals of political and economic control. When the military national educational reform for elementary and secondary schools first appeared (Lei de Diretrizes e Bases) in 1971, Brazilian education became politically arrested in a national curriculum for vocational schools and national programs of mass literacy, which demanded a love for the "Motherland." As Tomaz Tadeu da Silva and Peter McLaren (1993) clarify,

following the coup (backed by U.S. economic support and aid at the military and trade union level), the military government began a project of economic and social modernization, along with an intense political repression that included a suppression of civil liberties. In a wave of barbarism unprecedented in the country's history, thousands were arrested, tortured, or killed by both military and paramilitary assassination squads. Among the first to be targeted were priests, religious and lay persons active in movements for social change, and educators and university professors. In fact, education was one of the prime targets of the military government's crackdown. The educational policy of the military government included the following:

1. A rationalization and modernization of the universities [Educational reform of 1968]. The main lines of this project were drawn up through an agreement with USAID.
2. A campaign of mass literacy . . . which became known as MOBRAL (Movimento Brasileiro de Alfabetização) [Brazilian Movement of Literacy].
3. A project of reform of elementary and secondary education in order to fit the outcome of education to the manpower needs of a modernizing economy. (p. 37)

It was exactly within the reform of elementary and secondary education that Brazilian education became clearly connected to economic investment during the military years . However, vocational training was not only valued but also was an influential doctrine of moral and civic patriotism, taking the form of a subject matter called "Educação Moral e Cívica" (moral and civic education) at all levels of instruction. In graduate levels, this doctrine was hidden under the name "Estudos dos Problemas Brasileiros" (studies of Brazilian problems). Issuing from these perspectives was the military government's belief that the meaning of the words "Ordem e Progresso" (order and progress) emblazoned on the Brazilian flag could be fully reoriented. For this purpose, the population experienced not only the most terrible physical repression but also intellectual coercion. As I stated in an interview with Peter McLaren (1993a), "While I was an undergraduate student . . . my classmates and I experienced with a frightening intensity the oppressiveness of military power because we had military spies in our classroom and we could not talk about politics. We could not be seen with books considered 'dangerous,' such as Paulo Freire's books" (p. 313).

During the years of military dictatorship, Brazilian popular culture was all but silenced. For instance, my own generation, which was adolescent during the 1970s, was prepared to value U.S. music basically for two reasons: First, the majority of the Brazilian population did not know English. Second, U.S. music did not address any socio-political conflict that Brazilians were experiencing. At that time, Brazilian music was connected to the idea of subversion. It was a common practice that Brazilian composers and singers were arrested immediately following a TV show or a music festival because their music was considered politically subversive by the military government. In schools, students were encouraged to sing military anthems that reinforced a personal commitment to the Motherland through lyrics such as, "We are the motherland's guardians/ faithful soldiers loved by her."

Within the national educational reform of 1971, the teaching of a foreign language, especially English, was mandated throughout the country. However, second language instruction was always part of Brazilian educational curricula. Before the military years, second language instruction was mandated because the curriculum was connected to the ideals of a sophisticated European culture. At that time, students in middle and high schools studied not only modern languages such as French and English but also Latin. After 1971, second language instruction became focused on the acquisition of English because this language was considered relevant for an accurate reading of technical books that were considered important to vocational programs. Especially during the 1970s, students were told that to succeed professionally they should know English.

In Brazil, the idea of a national curriculum constitutes, in my opinion, one of the major educational weaknesses of the country, since a national curriculum fails to seriously consider the importance of local knowledges or any kind of cultural particularity and diversity. The sense that one curriculum is appropriate for all Brazilian states and municipalities denies the cultural complexities of a country that is multicultural in essence, one in which diversity is omnipresent. Despite the fact that there exists a myriad of educational attempts to alter the military vision of education, even after the end of the military years and the political conflicts of the beginning of the 1990s, with elected president Fernando Collor's impeachment, the national curriculum of 1971 is still the Brazilian national curriculum.

Educational changes are visible in some of the major cities and capitals of Brazilian states. For instance, the work developed by Paulo Freire as Secretary of Education in the municipality of São Paulo (1989–1991) connected to the movements of democratic socialism of the "Partido dos Trabalhadores" (Workers' Party) included the elaboration and expansion of critical literacy through a project called "Movimento para Alfabetização" (MOVA).[2] MOVA developed a political and social vision for literacy that was condemned during the military years. Furthermore, the work developed by Paulo Freire in his capacity as Secretary of Education improved not only student enrollment and retention but also teachers' salaries and conditions of work. Nevertheless, in the interior of Brazilian states, the military "Lei de Diretrizes e Bases" is the only educational policy that teachers and administrators know. In 1992, during my own experience working with teachers in the interior of Rio de Janeiro state, I could see they still believed in the ideological imperatives of military educational reform. The pseudo-national and single, white, heterosexual, and middle-class identity of Brazil is clearly maintained within their curriculum development. For instance, teachers still use textbooks in

---

2. For more details about MOVA and the work developed by Paulo Freire as Secretary of Education, see Carlos Alberto Torres and Paulo Freire's (1994), "Twenty years after *Pedagogy of the Oppressed*: Paulo Freire in conversation with Carlos Alberto Torres," in Peter McLaren and Colin Lankshear (eds.) *Politics of Liberation: Paths from Freire*.

which the Brazilian population is portrayed through images of people with blonde hair and blue eyes and with people who have the whole family at home sporting stylish middle-class clothes. African Brazilians are remembered in the curriculum in May when the anniversary of their official freedom (May 13, 1888) is celebrated and Native Brazilians are mentioned every April 19, which is called "Indian's Day." Furthermore, instructional exercises have little or no relation to students' lives—students who are, generally, very poor and work on farms after or before school. In rural areas of Rio de Janeiro state, teachers work with students of diverse grade levels in the same classroom. In some schools there is only one teacher who is responsible not only for teaching but also for the whole school building. The widespread teachers' belief in a curriculum that does not value students' local realities illustrates the powerful educational annihilation promoted during the military years and continuing to this day. Both teachers and students unwittingly reproduce the educational annihilation that maintains their oppression.

Brazil embraces a tremendous variety of ethnic groups. For instance, Martin Marger (1994) argues that

> whereas the United States maintains an essentially biracial system in which people are classified as either white or black [sic], Brazil's multiracial system provides for more than two categories. Three major racial groupings are recognized in Brazil, but the boundaries between them are neither rigid nor clear-cut. Branco (white), preto (black) [sic], and pardo (mulatto) are the most encompassing terms, but Brazilians employ literally dozens of more precise terms to categorize people of various mixed racial origins, depending on their physical features. . . . Miscegenation has, from the time of the initial Portuguese settlement, been a constant and widespread practice in Brazil among the society's three major population types—European, African, and Indian. . . . Although the boundaries of the three major groupings are not precise, there is little question that whites, mulattoes, and blacks [sic] represent a hierarchy of economic, political, and social standing. Whites are clearly at the top, followed in order by mulattoes and blacks [sic]. (pp. 441–445)

Because Brazil is a multicultural country without a multicultural education, I believe a new educational vision in Brazil is imperative. This vision must be one in which the diversity of the country is taken seriously in curriculum development. In fact, what is at stake is similar to the condition of students everywhere throughout the United States: Brazil needs to be challenged by a pedagogy that has the potential to develop a multicultural perspective for education. This vision directed my interest to the Bakhtin circle's theory since this theory is helpful not only to analyze the ways in which multicultural voices are socially juxtaposed but also to develop a broader understanding of their conflictual existence within the social and political arena.

The theory of Valentin Voloshinov represents a powerful insight into the way in which language teaching and learning are understood, especially in his book *Marxism and the Philosophy of Language*. However, there exists a strong debate surrounding the validity of Voloshinov as the sole author, not only of this book but also of other writings published under his name. Within this debate there are advocates of the idea that Valentin Voloshinov did not write the ideas presented in *Marxism and the Philosophy of Language* as well as in *Freudianism: A Marxist Critique*. Instead, these advocates believe that Mikhail Bakhtin, who was the leader of what came to be called *the Bakhtin circle*, was responsible for these books. Other groups of scholars believe that, despite the close friendship between Voloshinov and Bakhtin, Voloshinov was the only author responsible for the ideas suggested in these books. I will discuss this issue in more detail in chapter 1 of this book.

Voloshinov's theory challenges the structuralist conceptions of language, which address a distinction between 'langue' (individual act of communication) and 'parole' (communication in social settings), advocated by Ferdinand de Saussure and echoed at the present time in linguistic theories such as Noam Chomsky's.

Noam Chomsky (1965, 1981), one of the Saussure's followers, addresses the concepts of generative grammar and analyzes the relationship between 'competence' (the knowledge of the language system) and 'performance' (the use of competence in social communication), based on Saussure's distinction between langue and parole. The difference between these two linguists is that Chomsky rejects Saussure's assumption that langue is just a systematic inventory but he agrees with Saussure's (1959) explanation that "language is not a function of the speaker; it is a product that is passively assimilated by the individual" (p. 14). Furthermore, both Saussure and Chomsky believe the social arena has little impact on one's language. In other words, both linguists recognize the importance of the social environment but ratify the idea that language can be analyzed out-side of social constraints.

Contrary to Saussure's and Chomsky's theories, Voloshinov argues that there is no possible analysis of language without considering processes of social interaction. For example, Voloshinov (1973) asserts that any word is, first of all, an ideological phenomenon and that language is a social manifestation because it is socially constructed. Therefore, the theories addressed by Voloshinov challenge the concepts of structural linguistics, because linguists such as Saussure and Chomsky neglect the ideological environment within the process of acquiring a language. However, in the field of educational research, only a few scholars (e.g., Peter McLaren and Colin Lankshear, 1993; Richard Quantz and Terence O'Connor, 1988; Henry Giroux, 1988a) have recognized the relevance of Voloshinov's con-tributions to language.

The word *bilingual* means "two languages," but when we use the word *language* we cannot neglect the fact that a language embraces cul-tural, historical, and political dimensions. This means that when we ana-lyze a specific language and its expressions we are strongly connected to its social meanings. Therefore, in this book I will not use the conventional expression *bilingual–bicultural education*, because bilingual education must be understood in advance as biculturalism. However, there exists a ten-dency to overlook the relationship between linguistic performance (speech, reading, and writing) and social contexts (Marcia Moraes, 1992a; Jim Cummins, 1986). This lacunae in the literature and in bilingual edu-cation curricula has demonstrated that language teaching and learning are not associated with social and cultural meanings.

Since their first years in school, students are told emphatically that they have to write correctly; they have to read correctly; and they have to talk correctly. One question emerges from this context that seems particu-larly relevant: What does it mean to know and to be able to communicate "correctly" in a language? The meaning of correctly in schools has repre-sented and continues to serve as a form of domination in which the stan-dards of language are inextricably linked to the power of dominant groups. For instance, Lisa Delpit (1988) analyzes the culture of power that exists in society as well as in schools. Her analysis is located in a discussion of the ways in which nonstandard voices (e.g., African Americans and Native Alaskans) are overlooked in schools. According to Delpit's analysis, white educators possess the authority to establish the criteria for judging the 'truth' of research findings, regardless of the existing social makeup. This phenomenon incorporates predefined aspects of a standard culture that stems from dominant groups and serves as a means of stipulating the sense of what is appropriate or what is considered culturally correct. From this perspective, Delpit (1988) emphasizes that "students will be judged on their product regardless of the process they utilized to achieve it" (p. 287). In other words, correct ways of writing and reading in schools are inscribed as legitimating norms according to specific meanings that are meaningful only for a particular group. From this hegemonic process, especially in bilingual education, students are situated in a process of standardized memorization of vocabulary and grammatical correctness that does not draw upon their cultural background, their lived experiences, and their ethno-linguistic diversity. It follows, therefore, that language becomes reduced to a set of cognitive skills to be acquired in the absence of the students' social identity that delineates their ethnicity, their gender, and their class (Dennis Carlson, 1993a).

Since I advocate the importance of discussing language learning processes within multicultural perspectives, my hope is that the critical analysis that shapes this book may be helpful for educators, researchers, and theorists in the field of bilingual education. By uncovering the discursive regimes and social processes that inform practice, educators may develop a new perspective about how knowledge is created, legitimated, and mediated by its relationship with the larger society. Furthermore, from the theoretical perspectives addressed in this book, educational planners may reevaluate the curriculum development of bilingual programs. Current models of curriculum development based on competition, measurement, and accountability as a means of legitimating knowledge do not help foster the formation of students as active social and cultural agents imbued with a whole history of meanings and practices.

The purpose of chapter 1 is an analysis of Voloshinov's theory. My emphasis is directed at the ways in which Voloshinov theorizes about language and its relationship to social contexts. Because of the debate regarding the authorship of Voloshinov's publications, I also consider Bakhtin's perspectives on language. The major goal here is a broader understanding of the way in which the Bakhtin circle conceptualized language. This chapter represents the first step within one of the objectives of this book, which is a connection between the Bakhtin circle's theory and bilingual education. For this reason, the title of this book is *Bilingual Education: A Dialogue with the Bakhtin Circle.*

It is worth noting that the major assumptions of bilingual programs have arisen from the debates between English-only versus English-plus movements (Mary McGroarty, 1992). On the one hand, there are advocates of bilingual programs in which non-English speakers are encouraged to learn through their own language while at the same time are slowly introduced to English (English-plus movement). On the other hand, there are advocates of immersion programs that reinforce English learning while avoiding Spanish or any other non-English language in classrooms (English-only movement). Because of this existing debate, chapter 2 addresses a brief historical overview of bilingual education in the United States since 1966, when Anne Stemmler published her important article, "An Experimental Approach to the Teaching of Oral Language and Reading," in the *Harvard Educational Review*. Stemmler (1966) participated in one of the first educational research projects dealing with language development and reading skills of the "disadvantaged Spanish-speaking child in Texas" (p. 43). In this chapter, my attempt is to examine the ways in which federal policies and laws have had the effect of incorporating bilingual education with hegemonic discourses of ethnic uniformity rather than emancipatory cultural democracy. In this important sense, I agree with Peter McLaren's (1993b) assertion that "we should explore with more exigence how meanings and hegemonic articulations are manufactured" (p. 17).

The main focus of chapter 3 is a critical analysis of bilingual education research findings from the perspective of the epistemological assumptions of Voloshinov's and Bakhtin's (the Bakhtin circle) theory. This chapter also discusses existing theoretical approaches to second language acquisition and presents a brief analysis of Noam Chomsky's linguistic theory in light of the Bakhtin circle's philosophy of language.

From the perspectives addressed by the Bakhtin circle, 'dialogue' and 'otherness' represent key concepts of our social existence. Existence (as language) is forged within dialogic social interactions among people. Since we cannot deny our dialogic existence, chapter 4 is dedicated to a broader development of a pedagogy in which voices are not just heard or conscious of social constraints but work toward social hope and global empowerment. Here, the concept of dialogue developed by Paulo Freire and the social and political project of critical pedagogy addressed by critical educational theorists play a crucial role. Following this idea, chapter four analyzes the ways in which the theories of dialogism addressed by the Bakhtin circle and the theories of dialogue addressed by Freire can further advance the project of critical pedagogy toward a truly emancipatory democracy through a *dialogic-critical pedagogy.*

It worth noting that while the debate surrounding English-only versus English-plus has been largely restricted to linguistic performance (speech, reading, and writing) and disconnected from the crucial participation of language in social meanings, some scholars have addressed the needs of bilingual education as a part of multicultural education that promotes cultural and historical diversity, reflecting affirmative ethnicity and social identities (Luis Moll, 1992; bell hooks, 1993; Sonia Nieto, 1993; Peter McLaren, 1993c). Following this view, chapter 5 discusses the relevance of a dialogic-critical pedagogy, which has the potential of transforming the second language acquisition process into a more meaningful way of teaching and learning for both teachers and students. I understand this process to be one that is grounded in critical reflection by teachers and students toward a collective construction of transformative knowledge and emancipatory social practices. In this sense, knowledge must be viewed not as a limit, but as a means of ennoblement—of questioning, imagining, and formulating alternative social realities. My focus in chapter 5 is a discussion of the relevance of a dialogic-critical pedagogy for bilingual education, in which "difference" is not threatening but necessary to a social imagination that extends the meanings of human capacity and freedom.

The conclusion of this analysis is that a dialogic-critical pedagogy, based upon certain epistemological assumptions found in the work of the Bakhtin circle and Paulo Freire, offers the necessary theoretical grounds for the development of a more progressive model of bilingual and multicultural education. However, this book will limit its focus to bilingual education generally, as it applies to instances where one student has already one language well established before learning a second language.

In this book I will use the term "United Statian" to designate people who are citizens of the United States. Usually, the term "American" is used to name U.S. citizens. However, if we observe the English terminology for other American citizenship denominations (e.g., Mexican, Canadian, Brazilian) it seems appropriate to use the term "United Statian."

I understand that if I call U.S. citizens "Americans" I will be excluding other groups of citizens who are also Americans.

*We must renounce our monologic habits.*
— Bakhtin (1984, p. 272)

# CHAPTER ONE

# THE BAKHTIN CIRCLE
# AND LANGUAGE

*It is impossible to achieve greatness in one's*
*own time. Greatness always makes itself*
*known only to descendents, for whom such a*
*quality is always located in the past (it turns*
*into a distanced image); it has become an*
*object of memory and not a living object that*
*one can see and touch.*
　　　　　　　　　　　—Bakhtin (1981, p. 19)

Human history has shown that people who were interested in understanding human relations, its politics, its mechanisms of domination and subordination, and its social-ideological analysis, were condemned by the dominant ideology that is always affected when it is uncovered, denounced, and deconstructed. This is the history of many people who suffered persecution, imprisonment, exile, extermination, false assumptions of suicide, and so forth. This is, for instance, the history of Karl Marx, Paulo Freire, Rosa Luxemburg, Antonio Gramsci, and of many groups, including the Bakhtin circle.

The Russian philosopher, Mikhail Mikhailovich Bakhtin (1895–1975), can be considered one of the most important intellectuals of our century. As history shows, Bakhtin suffered persecution and exile during the 1920s and 1930s because, through his studies of social theory, poetics, and philosophy, he was uncovering the ways in which people are manipulated by dominant ideologies. Despite the persecution at that time, when the Soviet Union was facing revolution and repression, Bakhtin and other

13

scholars were together composing a group whose major goal was the discussion of philosophy and politics. The group was comprised, on a regular basis, of Bakhtin; Valentin Nikolaevich Voloshinov (linguist and musicologist); Pavel Nikolaevich Medvedev (literary theorist and editor of academic journals); and Lev Pumpianskij (philologist and professor of literature). However, there were many other scholars, including pianists, artistic directors, and archeologists who periodically attended the group discussions. Furthermore, it is supposed that works of intellectuals such as Lev Vygotsky were discussed among members of the Bakhtin circle since its members shared a myriad of theoretical assumptions addressed by Vygotsky—especially about social consciousness (Clark and Holquist, 1984).

I. R. Titunik, who is the translator of Voloshinov's *Marxism and the Philosophy of Language* (1973) as well as *Freudianism: A Marxist Critique* (1976), emphasizes the importance of the Bakhtin circle.

> Recently, thanks to the current phenomenal renaissance of semiotics in the Soviet Union, new and intriguing information has come to light concerning a whole school of semioticians operating during the period of the late 1920s and early 1930s. M. M. Baxtin, whose masterworks on Dostoevskij and Rabelais have now achieved international acclaim, has been identified as the leader of this school and V. N. Voloshinov as his closest follower and collaborator. (1973, p. 6)

Titunik (1973) explains that during the 1920s and 1930s there was a group of scholars who were investigating the theory of language and literature in the field of semiology. The translator argues that this group not only had Mikhail Bakhtin as a leader but was also interested in a Marxian study of ideologies—which always represented a threat to any established political system. As a result of the pressures that stemmed from the political constraints at that time, Katerina Clark and Michael Holquist (1984) inform us that

> Bakhtin was arrested around January 7, 1929, on a number of charges. One charge, which was later dropped, was that of being a member of the Brotherhood of Saint Serafim. Another charge was that a list of members of a future anti-Communist Russian government, published in Paris, included his name. . . . Still another charge was that in his private lectures in the pastoral

courses around Leningrad Bakhtin had engaged in the Socratic crime of 'corrupting the young.' (p. 142)

In fact, there exists considerable information about Bakhtin (e.g, Clark and Holquist, 1984; Hirschkop, 1989), but very little information about his friends and the way in which the circle internally operated. What is known is that the principal members of the Bakhtin circle during the 1920s—Valentin Voloshinov, Pavel Medvedev, and Mikhail Bakhtin—shared certain assumptions: that social interaction constructs meanings and that language both represents and masks ideologies. But the general lack of information about the Bakhtin circle limits a broader understanding of the role played in the circle by Medvedev, for instance, or even by Voloshinov, who published books based on Marxian analysis. Some scholars presume that Voloshinov disappeared in the Stalinist purge during the 1930s (Ponzio, 1990). Other scholars believe that Voloshinov died in the beginning of the 1930s as a victim of tuberculosis without finishing his works and that Medvedev died in the beginning of the 1940s in a unknown place after he was arrested in 1938 (Clark and Holquist, 1984). Many scholars (e.g., Wehrle, 1978; Holquist, 1990; Walsh, 1991) believe that Bakhtin is the author of books and articles published under Voloshinov's and Medvedev's names. However, in every assumption about the disputed texts, there is no final answer to the ongoing debate about the authorship of these texts.

## VOLOSHINOV OR BAKHTIN? WHOSE AUTHORSHIP?

The question "Whose authorship?" was transformed into an extensive debate that attempted to clarify whether or not Valentin Voloshinov's books were written by Mikhail Bakhtin. On the one hand, there are advocates of Bakhtin as the only author despite the recognition that Voloshinov was interested in a semiotic analysis of Marxian views. On the other hand, there are advocates of Voloshinov's authorship. Among many scholars, these two groups of advocates have been strongly represented by I. R Titunik, who believes that Bakhtin is not the author under Voloshinov's name, and Katerina Clark and Michael Holquist, who believe that the works published under Voloshinov's name are Bakhtin's complete authorship.

The group that is favorable to Bakhtin's authorship believes that because of the political and social pressure of the 1920s and 1930s in the Soviet Union, among other reasons, Bakhtin published *Marxism and the Philosophy of Language* and *Freudianism: A Marxist Critique* under the authorship of Voloshinov. For instance, Katerina Clark and Michael Holquist (1984) dedicated a whole chapter of their book to discuss this authorship issue.

> Voloshinov's first wife flatly disavows her husband's authorship and claims that Bakhtin wrote the two books in question. . . . One objection raised to Bakhtin's authorship is the difficulty of writing four books [Medvedev and Voloshinov's books], each covering a different field, and several articles all during the brief period from 1926 to 1929. In reality, however, these works were merely published during that period and were actually written over a much longer period. . . . Most of the conditions of Bakhtin's life in the late 1920s were also conducive to productivity. He had no children and few job obligations. . . . Although Bakhtin was chronically ill, he had a remarkable intellectual energy, which lasted until the end of his life. Indeed, the explanation he gave to Yudina as to why he had published under his friends' names included the statement: 'We were friends. We would discuss things. But they had their jobs, while I had the time to write.' (pp. 148–149)

Furthermore, in their analysis of Bakhtin's work, Clark and Holquist (1984) emphasize the connection of Bakhtin to Marxism. They believe that, despite the general belief that Bakhtin was not a Marxian, Bakhtin used Marxian terminology and theoretical aspects such as the powerful ideologies of capitalism in Russia in many of his published works. In other words, Clark and Holquist believe that Bakhtin was always able to connect his own thoughts to Marxian political and social positions. However, these explanations and other explanations presented by Clark and Holquist do not seem sufficient to convince Titunik that this is proof of Bakhtin's authorship. Despite the intellectual bond with Voloshinov during the period of the Bakhtin circle's existence, Titunik does not believe that Bakhtin has written Voloshinov's published works.

In 1986, two years after the publication of Clark and Holquist's *Mikhail Bakhtin*, an open forum appears in the *Slavic and East European Journal* to discuss the relevance of Bakhtin's work. In this forum, the authorship issue comes into play and Titunik, Clark, and Holquist went back to the extensive debate, in which the main point is the connection between Marxism and Bakhtin's theoretical reflections. However, despite the discussion among these scholars, it is incontestable within this forum that none of them has the final answer to the authorship debate. On the one hand, Titunik (1986) criticizes Clark and Holquist's assumptions because they simply connect the relationship between Bakhtin and Marxism on the basis of the use of Marxian terminology in publications under Bakhtin's name. In other words, Titunik does not believe that Marxian terminology in Bakhtin's work is a sufficient explanation to consider Bakhtin as a Marxian. Furthermore, Titunik (1986) argues that

> [w]e are told that Voloshinov wrote a dissertation topic of which 'was probably the problem of how to present reported speech' (110). As the authors well know, a whole section (part 3) of Voloshinov's *Marksizm i filosofija jazyka* is devoted precisely to the problem of reported speech. Are the two items one and the same? Clark and Holquist inexplicably did not investigate. . . . The whole issue of the authorship and/or responsibility of/for the disputed texts is perplexing; it is a riddle which has not been solved . . . but nothing I have read in that book has persuaded me to alter the attitude of skepticism. . . . The circumstantial evidence for attribution of the disputed texts to Baxtin is formidable. But merely to assign everything to Baxtin and to consign Voloshinov and Medvedev to oblivion—the tack taken by the majority of interested parties including Clark and Holquist—is not only manifestly unfair but also does not eliminate the problem. (pp. 93–94)

This critique against Clark's and Holquist's assumptions addressed by Titunik is shared with Gary Saul Morson (1986), who argues that the authorship issue became a comparison of intellectual ability and intelligence among the Bakhtin circle members. Morson (1986) asserts that

> Clark and Holquist also contend that the undisputed texts of Volosinov are of a lower quality, and the undisputed texts of Medvedev of a much lower quality than the undisputed texts of Baxtin, and, therefore that Volosinov, and especially Medvedev, were not intelligent enough to have written anything but the poorer passages of Marxism, Freudianism, and The Formal

Method. . . . One might also add that judgments about the quality of a work are notoriously subjective and unreliable. (p. 87)

On the other hand, Clark and Holquist (1986) argue that they did not assume a final position regarding the disputed texts. However, they respond to Titunik's analysis.

> He [Titunik] asks if the portions of *Marxism and the Philosophy of Language* devoted to [reported speech] are not identical to Voloshinov's dissertation on the same topic, a question which 'Clark and Holquist inexplicably did not investigate.' That we cannot answer this question does not mean we did not investigate it. The fact is, Voloshinov did not finish the dissertation and no copy of his notes remains. . . . Another aspect of our book that troubles Titunik, and for which a definitive answer cannot be provided, is the account we give of Baxtin's relation to Marxism. . . . There is every reason to believe Baxtin was never a Marxian in any conventional sense of that word . . . but to say as much is not to deny that Marx may have been an important influence in Baxtin's development. Baxtin was in sympathy with Marxism's emphasis on collective over individual factors in society, and he was impressed by the notion of the ineluctability of historical struggle between those having power and those without it. (p. 98)

It is obvious that a final answer to the authorship debate does not exist. For this reason, I would like to clarify what my own position is in this debate. As we could read in the previous paragraphs of this brief section, there exists a lack of evidence to explain whether or not Bakhtin wrote the published works under Voloshinov's name. Regarding the authorship debate, I completely agree with Ken Hirschkop (1989a) who argues that

> we have to confront what might seem to be rather a pedantic issue: how and by whom were the texts published under the names of Medvedev and Voloshinov written? This problem has had an ambiguous effect on Bakhtin scholarship. On the whole it has clearly been an obstacle to interesting work on Bakhtin and company, because it has licensed a shift of attention away from the theoretical and historical issues posed in the texts to questions about the lives and personal motivations of the

authors. But this question of attribution is made more interesting by the fact that it is so obviously a political question as well.
The writings of Voloshinov and Medvedev attack the same
problems with much the same weapons as the writings of
Bakhtin, and each of these texts can be read as a gloss on the
others. (p. 196)

Therefore, I will consider that Valentin Voloshinov is the author of
*Marxism and the Philosophy of Language* as well as *Freudianism: A Marxist
Critique*. On the other hand, there exists evidence (e.g., Titunik, 1973,
1986; Wehrle, 1978; Clark and Holquist, 1984, 1986; Morson and
Emerson, 1989) that Mikhail Bakhtin and Valentin Voloshinov belonged
to the same group of scholars who studied the interconnections between
language and society. For this reason, I will also consider Bakhtin's theory
in the context of a broader understanding of the way in which the Bakhtin
circle conceptualized language.


## THE WORLD OF LANGUAGE THROUGH
## VOLOSHINOV'S AND BAKHTIN'S EYES

Voloshinov argues that the main aspect in the Marxian analysis of ideologies is the interrelationship between base and superstructure, that is, an
analysis of what constitutes society in the light of human relations. In fact,
the explanation of this interrelationship is completely connected to an
understanding of the philosophy of language because it is the domain of
ideology that has the possibility of changing social relations. It is through
language, among many processes, that a material representation of culture
and history of humankind as a social agent is established. For this reason,
Voloshinov (1973) understands the philosophy of language as "the philosophy of the ideological sign" (p. 15). In this sense, language is conceptualized as a semiotic social entity that exists within the domain of ideologies.
Furthermore, in order to explain psychological processes as social,
Voloshinov (1973, 1976) articulates the relationship between sign and ideology, demonstrating that the analysis addressed by linguists and psychologists is merely focused on written systematization without looking at the
social and ideological aspects of the sign.

## Sign

Voloshinov (1973) argues that when a tool is created it has a specific function of production. However, a tool is not itself a sign but it can be converted into an ideological sign when 'treated'. For instance, there are different colors and many stars in the Brazilian flag: blue represents the sky, green represents the forests, white represents peace, yellow represents the gold and precious stones of the land, and each star represents one of the Brazilian states. Another example is that while we are driving, we know that we should stop when the light is red and we can move on when the light is green. Here, we are perceiving different signals (colors) that have become signs (ideological meaning). This means that anything can be an ideological sign that goes beyond the primary meaning. For this reason, Voloshinov (1973) argues that everything in an artistic-symbolic image is an ideological product converted into a sign. However, the existence of a social organization is necessary for the composition of an ideological sign. The ideological sign, thus, is a source of communication among people since the social material of signs is created by humans. There is no society without signs and a sign does not exist outside of society.

The ideological phenomena are connected to the conditions and forms of social communication, and signs are determined by this communication. In fact, a sign represents communication in a material form. When a sign is presented, ideology is presented, therefore, everything ideological contains semiotic value. This means that a sign is an embodiment of ideology. Ideology becomes a semiotic material in order to guarantee its own existence. According to Bakhtin (1981), our experiences are completely social and the ideological takes the form of a sign, which remains something that we can see or hear. Furthermore, every ideological sign is created within temporal and spatial structures that will never exist outside of social life. In this way, individual consciousness can only understand ideology and signs from the perspective of social interaction.

One of the major Voloshinov's arguments is that any word is an ideological phenomenon. The word has a function of a sign and, therefore, exists within social interaction. However, signs and symbols are created within a specific field and have specific ideological function, while the word can transport any kind of ideological function. For this reason, Voloshinov argues that a word is a neutral sign because a word can be used in any field, in a myriad of ideological functions. However, once a word is placed in a field, in a social context, it loses its neutrality, as Bakhtin (1981) argues: "[A]ll words have the 'taste' of a profession, a genre, a tendency, a party, a particular work, a particular person, a generation, an age group, the day and hour. Each word tastes of the context and contexts in which it has lived its socially charged life" (p. 293). Therefore, a word is not only the material of communication but is also permeated by a myriad of purposes, of social intentions.

For Voloshinov (1973), a word plays the role of "the semiotic material of inner life—of consciousness (inner speech)" (p. 14) because a word is created by humans without any kind of extra corporeal material. However, a word is the materialization of inner engagement. In this way, Voloshinov (1973) argues that "individual consciousness as the inner word (as an inner sign in general) becomes one of the most vital problems in philosophy of language" (p. 14). He also says a word is more than a social sign because a word is also a medium of consciousness. This means consciousness can be developed because a word is the necessary material that makes possible the existence of consciousness.

Because inner speech (the semiotic material of inner life—of consciousness) plays a crucial role in the process of understanding any kind of ideological phenomenon (painting, music, human behavior, etc.), even nonverbal signs cannot be disconnected from speech. This does not mean a word can replace an ideological sign but that each ideological sign is always supported and also accompanied by words. For instance, when we are driving in a car we see the color red and it means "stop." Therefore, cultural signs in our social life become part of the verbally constituted aspect of consciousness because there is always the presence of word when we understand or interpret anything.

Voloshinov's theory asserts the word is not only an ideological phenomenon but is also an index of social changes because the word registers the transition in each phase of social change, including its own participation in the production of ideological forms. Let's analyze how this happens.

To begin with, the ideological sign is determined by an intersection of different social interests. Voloshinov (1973) says that "each and every word is ideological and each and every application of language involves ideological change" (p. 94). This means the ideological sign represents an arena of class struggle in society because diverse classes will use one specific language (English, for instance) but every ideological sign is fulfilled with different accents—accents that belong to people's social locations. Bakhtin (1981) argues that accents represent a vital characteristic of stratification of language.

[T]hese languages [the language of the lawyer, the doctor, the businessman, the politician, the public education teacher and so forth] differ from each other not only in their vocabularies; they involve specific forms for manifesting intentions, forms for making conceptualization. . . . What is important to us here is the intentional dimensions, that is, the denotative and expressive dimension of the "shared" language's stratification. It is in fact not the neutral linguistic components of language being stratified, but rather a situation in which the intentional possibilities of language are being expropriated: these possibilities are realized in specific directions, filled with specific content, they are made concrete, particular, and are permeated with concrete value judgments. (p. 289)

For this reason, Voloshinov remarks that any ideological accents are, in fact, social accents since it claims to social recognition. Consequently, the main aspect of the sign is its relevance within inter-groups relationships. In this sense, Bakhtin points out that the stratification of language is, in fact, social stratification, since the foreigners/outsiders who are not engaged in such professional jargons are excluded from the intentionality of these languages. Therefore, individual consciousness enters into a process to assimilate all of the social accents of ideological signs. This is what Voloshinov calls *multiaccentuality*, which emerges, basically, in social struggles. In other words, multiaccentuality represents an encounter of diverse social accents. Voloshinov's idea of multiaccentuality within any language is described as *heteroglossia* in Bakhtin's words. Bakhtin (1981) argues that

at any given moment of its historical existence, language is heteroglot from top to bottom: it represents the co-existence of socio-ideological contradictions between the present and the past, between differing epochs of the past, between different socio-ideological groups in the present, between tendencies, schools, circles and so forth. . . . Each of these 'languages' of heteroglossia requires a methodology very different from the others . . . all languages of heteroglossia, whatever the principle underlying them and making each unique, are specific points of view on the world, forms for conceptualizing the world in words, specific world views, each characterized by its own objects, meanings and values. (pp. 291–292)

This multiaccentuality (or heteroglossia) is what makes an ideological sign not only something that is socially crucial but also something that is mutable within the social arena.

Beyond the multiaccentuality within any language, humans live in what Bakhtin calls a 'polyglot world'. The issue of a polyglot world is not a variety of existing languages but how a specific language exists in relation to other languages, how a specific dialect exists in relation to other dialects, and so forth. Bakhtin (1981) calls our attention to linguistic relationships in the world when he remarks that

> one language can, after all, see itself only in the light of another language. . . . [T]hat is, there is no more peaceful co-existence between territorial dialects, social and professional dialects and jargons, literary language, generic languages within literary language, epochs in language and so forth. All this set into motion a process of active, mutual cause-and-effect and interillumination. . . . [E]ach given language—even if its linguistic composition (phonetics, vocabulary, morphology, etc.) were to remain absolutely unchanged—is, as it were, reborn, becoming qualitatively a different thing for the consciousness that creates it. (p. 12)

Bakhtin's main point in the above quotation concerns the location of consciousness and what makes language an accentuated system that establishes marks for this location. Therefore, it is relevant that we can understand the process of consciousness existence—human consciousness that exists as social resonance.

*Consciousness*

Voloshinov believes the individual consciousness is constructed through social-ideological facts. He also argues that it is impossible for there to exist an objective definition of consciousness as well as an objective definition for unconsciousness. For Voloshinov, nobody can understand consciousness as an isolated form of thinking. He argues that "the only possible objective definition of consciousness is a sociological one. . . . The logic of consciousness is the logic of ideological communication, of the semiotic interaction of a social group" (1973, p. 13). This is the main critique Voloshinov addresses regarding Freud's analysis of consciousness and unconsciousness. Voloshinov argues that, in fact, Freud analyzed what he called the unconscious level through the conscious level of his patients. In Voloshinov's words, "Freud's whole psychological construct is based fundamentally on human verbal utterances; it is nothing but a special kind of interpretation of utterances. All these utterances are, of course, constructed in the conscious sphere" (1976, p. 76). This means that if we are going to talk about our dreams or fears, for instance, we have to talk about them through verbal utterances that exist in conscious time. Therefore, any assumption about our dreams or our fears is already impregnated with our social consciousness.

Once we are talking to someone else, we consider our social relations, and from these relationships we choose a verbal expression that seems to be more adequate for the situation. In other words, every verbal utterance illustrates the limits imposed by social-ideological intercourse within our lives. Even when we try to explain what happened while we were in an "unconscious time," we express everything through the content of our consciousness. Therefore, as Voloshinov (1976) argues, "The Freudian unconscious does not fundamentally differ from consciousness; it is only another form of consciousness, only an ideologically different expression of it" (p. 85). I believe that even if an individual is hypnotized, a common practice to reach one's unconscious level, everything that is said during a hypnosis session comes out through verbal expressions and, therefore, social consciousness. Everything in what Freud calls "unconsciousness" has a verbal expression which is, in fact, the verbal expressions of dreams, desires, impulses, fears, feelings, and so on. Once it becomes a verbal expression, it is consciousness. Consequently, everything that composes this utterance (e.g., words, intonation) is a whole social entity.

Voloshinov argues that, in order to understand consciousness, it is important to consider the Marxian analysis of ideologies. That is, we have to consider the existing social-ideological systems such as religion, laws, morality, science, art, and so forth, in which humans are inserted. All of these systems are what construct both inner (inner life of consciousness) and outward (oral or written) speech, as well as any kind of perception or action we can have. Voloshinov (1976) states:

> An experience of which an individual is conscious is already ideological and, therefore, from a scientific point of view, can in no way be a primary and irreducible datum; rather, it is an entity that has already undergone ideological processing of some spe-

cific kind. The haziest content of consciousness of the primitive savage and the most sophisticated cultural monument are only extreme links in the single chain of ideological creativity. . . . What is more, *my thought will be able to achieve final clarity only when I find exact verbal formulation for it.* . . . [H]uman consciousness operates through words—that medium which is the most sensitive and at the same time the most complicated refraction of the socioeconomic governance. [emphasis added] (p. 87)

Both ideological phenomena and individual consciousness exist only in relation to social organization and in the context of social interrelations. Since humans are social creatures, everything classified as psychological aspects are, in fact, social responses within human existence. Voloshinov (1976) argues that "there is no fundamental dividing line between the content of the individual psyche and formulated ideology" (p. 87). Therefore, there is no distinction between the psychological and social aspects of one's life. To illustrate this analysis, Bakhtin (1981) writes about the effects of people's words in our lives. The main point of his analysis is that we perceive ourselves through the lenses of other's words.

[P]eople talk most of all about what others talk about—they transmit, recall, weigh and pass judgment on other people's words, opinions, assertions, information; people are upset by others' words, or agree with them, contest them, refer to them and so forth. Were we to eavesdrop on snatches of raw dialogue in the street, in a crowd, in lines, in a foyer and so forth, we would hear how often the words 'he says,' 'people say,' 'he said . . .' are repeated. . . . [These repetitions] reflect how enormous is the weight of 'everyone says' and 'it is said' in public opinion, public rumor, gossip slander and so forth. (p. 338)

Bakhtin remarks about the ways in which others' words exert a powerful effect within our lives and the ways in which we give importance to understanding and interpreting others' words. This engagement among people within a network of transmission represents a social conceptual system that shapes our social existence. Therefore, we cannot separate what is psychological from what is social, because what is considered psychological is equally a social response. However, there exists a misunderstanding regarding the differences between what is natural and what is social in one's life. Voloshinov (1973) clarifies this distinction which, he says, has been misunderstood by psychologists and philosophers.

> To avoid misunderstanding, a rigorous distinction must always be made between the concept of the individual as natural speci-men without reference to the social world (i.e., the individual as object of the biologist's knowledge and study), and the concept of individuality, which has the status of an ideological-semiotic superstructure over the natural individual and which, therefore, is a social concept. (p. 34)

From Voloshinov's words we can perceive that consciousness exists only within the process of social interaction, which creates the ideological content. The ideological content is present in any word, in any utterance. It is around the concept of utterance that the whole idea of language as a vital social domain of ideologies is developed by the Bakhtin circle.

### Utterance

Since signs are social-ideological constructions and a word is a sign, Voloshinov argues that utterance can be only understood as a social phenomenon. That is, language is not an isolated phenomenon but a phenomenon that has its roots, creation, and existence within social relations. Furthermore, he argues that "[a]ny utterance, no matter how weighty and complete in and of itself, is only a moment in the continuous process of verbal communication. But that continuous verbal communication is, in turn, itself only a moment in the continuous all-inclusive, generative process of a given social collective" (1973, p.95). An utterance exists within this generative process of any social collective because every utterance is not only part of a language but, as Bakhtin asserts, it is also part of a social and historical heteroglossia (multiaccentuality).

Any utterance has its *theme*, *meaning*, and *evaluative accent*. Voloshinov (1973) argues that "the theme [of an utterance] is the expression of the concrete, historical situation that engendered the utterance" (p. 99). This means that any utterance has different meanings and themes, depending on the situation in which it is used. However, meaning and theme coexist within an utterance and this means that one does not exist without the other. The *theme* is composed of aspects of the situation in which an utterance is used. Nobody can understand the theme of an utterance if the moment (situation) is not taken into account.

Despite the impossibility of disconnecting what is meaning from what is theme in an utterance, Voloshinov (1973) argues that a theme is a concrete part of an utterance (such as the concrete moment in which an utterance is used), while meaning is what allows the accomplishment of a theme because meaning in an utterance is, in fact, a set of meanings altogether composing elements that are passive of reproduction in all instances of repetition. *Meaning* is what makes possible the existence of a theme because meaning is a composition of signs that are appropriate to the specific situation in which an utterance is used. Furthermore, beyond the fact that meaning makes possible the existence of the theme in an utterance, Voloshinov (1973) explains that "meaning belongs to a word according to its position between speakers. . . . *Meaning is the effect of interaction between speaker and listener*" [emphasis added] (p. 102). The social arena is what brings meaning to any utterance. Therefore, an utterance does not belong to someone but to this social arena where we are just social agents.

Beyond the presence of theme and meaning in any utterance, there exists also what Voloshinov calls *evaluative accent*. The evaluative accent in an utterance is the value judgment that permeates all words and all utterances. There is no one single word or utterance without evaluative accent, and this value judgment is permeated with social standpoints because the social arena is what will shape the way in which we evaluate everything.

Bakhtin (1981) writes that "the authentic environment of an utterance, the environment in which it lives and takes shape, is dialogized heteroglossia, anonymous and social as language, but simultaneously concrete, filled with specific content as an individual utterance" (p. 272). It is worth noting that every utterance has its meaning and its value. However, changes in meanings mean changes in values or reevaluation. In other words, when a specific word is transported to another context there is a change of meaning, there is a change in the evaluative accent (value judgment). Bakhtin (1981) explains this process:

[A]ny concrete discourse (utterance) finds the object at which it was directed already as it were overlain with qualifications, open to dispute, charged with value, already enveloped in an obscuring mist. . . . The living utterance, having taken meaning and shape at a particular historical moment in a socially specific environment, cannot fail to brush up against thousands of living dialogic threads, woven by socio-ideological consciousness around the given object of an utterance. (p. 276)

Utterances do not exist outside of living interaction. Utterances are confronted with other utterances and the social arena is composed of a social background facing another social background. In other words, in society, an utterance does not express isolated linguistic aspects. Contrarily, an utterance expresses diverse social backgrounds accompanied by diverse value judgments. It is in the confrontation among social backgrounds that an utterance exists with its meaning and theme. Therefore, the relevance of theme and meaning and the way in which both theme and meaning operate in an utterance constitute crucial aspects of the process of understanding of one's life—a process that is, in essence, dialogic.

### Process of Understanding

Voloshinov explains that the process of *understanding* cannot be misunderstood for the process of *recognizing*. In order to highlight this distinction Voloshinov maintains that we can recognize the linguistic form, but to understand this linguistic form it must be placed in a context. This is the difference between 'signal' and 'sign' (e.g., the color green—a signal—which became a sign in the Brazilian flag). A signal has no relation to the ideological unless it is placed in a context, in which case it becomes a sign. For instance, Voloshinov (1973) argues that the 'understander' is not attached to a linguistic form just because this individual uses the same language as other people in the community. To the understander, every sign is changeable and the process of understanding is not a mere recognition of the same thing but "understanding in the proper sense of the word, that is, orientation in the particular, given context and in the particular, given situation—orientation in the dynamic process of becoming and not 'orientation' in some inert state" (p. 69).

The relevant aspect of Voloshinov's analysis is that the process of understanding never exists outside of human ideology and behavior. He explains that the process of understanding is, in fact, an engagement within our lived ideological and behavioral context. Our behavior exists within ideological systems (art, religion, laws, etc.) that, in turn have a powerful influence upon our verbal reactions. For Voloshinov, the lack of this interpretation constitutes the most critical oversight committed by the advocates of abstract objectivism (Ferdinand de Saussure and his followers—whose theory I will discuss later in this chapter) because they do not recognize that a speaker's consciousness is a consciousness stemming from an ideological-social context in which each individual is inserted. There is no speaker's consciousness without social intercourse. Therefore, Voloshinov emphasizes that a system of language with immutable forms does not really exist, except in the abstract.

Bakhtin reinforces Voloshinov's analysis when he argues that an active understanding is a process in which a word is considered within a whole system of interrelationships. That is, a word is not understood in itself but in relation to a speaker's and listener's conceptual systems; that is, within a dialogic relationship in which understanding and response exist together. For this reason, Bakhtin (1981) argues that an utterance can be understood neither as a grammatical composition of words nor as a sentence out of context, and he clarifies the difference between *passive* and *active* understanding as follows:

> A *passive understanding* of linguistic meaning is no understanding at all, it is only the abstract aspect of meaning. But even . . . an understanding of the speaker's intention insofar as that understanding remains purely passive, purely receptive, contributes nothing new to the word under consideration. . . . Thus an *active understanding* . . . establishes a series of complex interrelationships, consonances and dissonances with the word and enriches it with new elements. [emphasis added] (pp. 281–282)

The difference between passive and active understanding is that active understanding includes the conceptual systems of both speaker and hearer. The speaker leaves words in the conceptual territory of the hearer who brings a responsive understanding to the elements that have just been received. At the same time, the speaker knows that any elements directed to the listener are of a passive response even when this response cannot be orally verbalized. Therefore, the dialogic relationship between speaker and listener is not a mere classification of linguistic style but, as Bakhtin points out, an exchange of consciousness. Furthermore, Voloshinov always remarks that any kind of understanding is dialogic in nature, because the process of understanding requires active responses within a context. Understanding is a process that comprises word and counter-word. That is, the encounter of conceptual systems in any kind of communication.

## Communication

The main purpose of language is to facilitate social interaction because language establishes relationships among people. Voloshinov (1973) argues that verbal interaction is the primary reality of any language. In fact, language is a vehicle for the construction of ideology and, therefore, is the product of ideological conception.

When writing about verbal communication, Voloshinov is not simply arguing that verbal communication is the oral part of language or that it is written material. The main aspect of verbal intercourse is that it coexists with other kinds of communication. That is, verbal communication

> is always accompanied with social acts of a nonverbal character (the performance of labor, the symbolic acts of a ritual, a ceremony, etc.), and is often only an accessory to these acts, merely carrying out an auxiliary role. Language acquires life and historically evolves precisely here, in concrete verbal communication, and not in the abstract linguistic system of language forms, nor in the individual psyche of speakers. (Voloshinov, 1973, p. 95)

This is to say that language must be perceived as a site of social-ideological existence in which the extraverbal context must be taken into account at the very moment of communication. Regarding the extraverbal context of an utterance and the primordial role of this context in communication, Voloshinov (1976) provides the following example:

> Two people are sitting in a room. They are both silent. Then one of them says, 'Well!' The other does not respond. For us, as outsiders, this entire 'conversation' is utterly incomprehensible. . . . We lack the 'extraverbal context'. . . . At the time the colloquy took place, both interlocutors *looked up* at the window and *saw* that it had begun to snow . . . *both were sick and tired* of the protracted winter . . . and both were bitterly disappointed by the late snowfall. . . . And yet all this remains without verbal specification or articulation [author's emphasis] (p. 99)

As Voloshinov points out, even if we could analyze the word *well* in its morphological or phonetic characteristics, we could never understand the utterance just because we did not understand the contextual aspects in which this single word was applied. Only after understanding the contextual overview in which the conversation took place and the ways in which both speakers/hearers were engaged, can we understand the meaning these speakers bring to the word well. In order for a responsive understanding to occur, the spoken "Well!" became more than a single word or an adverb followed by a punctuation mark. Therefore, an utterance exists within what is spoken and what is not spoken. This means that in any kind of communication, utterances exist in a context composed of space where the utterance is used; the speaker's understanding of a specific situation; and the speaker's evaluation of this situation. For this reason, Voloshinov (1973) is emphatic when he criticizes linguists because their attention (especially in the case of the representatives of abstract objectivism) has been directed to categories of language (e.g., morphological, syntactic) without considering utterance as a whole social entity. For instance, he argues that their definition of a sentence is implicit in an absurd assumption of monologic utterance. Furthermore, they consider morphological and syntactic categories of language as mutually exclusive when, in fact, these categories cannot exist. For Voloshinov, theme, meaning, and evaluative accent interexist in any utterance and utterances coexist with utterances. Therefore, an utterance cannot be considered within a monologic context.

Voloshinov (1973) argues that the main characteristic of communication resides in the phenomenon of the *reported speech*. He notes that reported speech is "speech within speech, utterance within utterance, and at the same time also speech about speech, utterance about utterance" (1973, p. 115). He also argues that it is impossible to disconnect *reported speech* from *reporting context*. Let's clarify his perspective.

What is important about reported speech is understanding the interconnection of reported speech and reporting context. The main issue is the way in which the reception of a reported utterance occurs. That is, the ways in which the reception of a speaker's speech exists in another speaker's speech. For instance, Voloshinov (1973) makes clear that one of the functions of society is a selection and adaptation of language factors in a grammatical structure exactly because the active and evaluative receptions are grounded within economic existence of individuals in a community. Receptions of any utterance are socially essential and continual. These receptions enter into an arena of mutable conflict because speakers of a particular community share diverse perspectives and, still, we socially live within this variety of tendencies. In other words, the main aspect of reported speech is its reception in speech itself—the social tendencies of reception in another speaker's speech. As I stated before, language does not exist outside of social interrelations. In this sense, Bakhtin (1981) clarifies this process of reception.

> The word in living conversation is directly, blatantly, oriented toward a future answer-word: it provokes an answer, anticipates it and structures itself in the answer's direction. Forming itself in an atmosphere of the already spoken, the word is at the same time determined by that which has not yet been said but which is needed and in fact anticipated by the answering word. Such is the situation in any living dialogue. (p. 280)

Therefore, there are no boundaries between reported speech and reporting context. What occurs is a dynamic inner-speech reception where word meets word within an active understanding in which the discourse is enriched, modified, and challenged. This is what constitutes the meaning of dialogue—an encounter among utterances; an encounter of one speech with another speech.

It is obvious that the key aspect of all of these theories addressed by the Bakhtin circle is not only the way in which ideologies are created but the relationship between ideology and consciousness. In this way, language is a whole social entity that embodies ideologies within our social existence or, in other words, *language is the way in which ideology becomes concrete.* Communication is, in essence, a social activity and no meaning of a word can be understood outside of this social recognition. This is the main critique addressed by Voloshinov regarding the theoretical assumptions advocated by Ferdinand de Saussure. Voloshinov (1973) argues that when linguists attempt to analyze language and its structures, they often lose the social dimension, which is the primary reason for the existence of language.

## A DEBATE BETWEEN VOLOSHINOV AND SAUSSURE: WHAT IS LANGUAGE?

As I stated in the introduction of this book, Voloshinov's and Bakhtin's theories represent a challenge to a structuralist/objectivist conception of language as addressed by Ferdinand de Saussure and echoed, at the present time, in the work of linguists such as Noam Chomsky—whose theories I will address in chapter 3 of this book. This dichotomy between these two groups of theorists lies in the sense that the first group—the Bakhtin circle—does not believe in linguistic analysis outside social relations, while the second group—Saussure and his followers—believes that language as a system can be analyzed outside human interrelations.

By the time the Bakhtin circle was developing studies in the philosophy of language, the theories developed by Ferdinand de Saussure and his students (who published his works after his death) represented a powerful movement that placed linguistics within a scientific understanding. Charles Bally and Albert Sechehaye (Saussure's students) were responsible for the first edition of Saussure's *Course in General Linguistics* in 1915. They write:

All those who had the privilege of participating in his richly rewarding instruction regretted that no book had resulted from it. After his death, we hoped to find in his manuscripts, obligingly made available to us by Mme. de Saussure, a faithful or at least an adequate outline of his inspiring lectures. At first we thought that we might simply collate F. de Saussure's personal notes and the notes of his students. We were misled. . . . As soon as they had served their purpose, F. de Saussure destroyed the rough drafts of the outlines used for his lectures. . . . We had to fall back on the notes collected by students during the course of his three series of lectures. Very complete notebooks were placed at our disposal. . . . We reached a bolder but also, we think, a more rational solution: to attempt a reconstruction, a synthesis, by using the third course as a starting point and by using all other materials at our disposal, including the personal notes of F. de Saussure, as supplementary sources. . . . From this work of assimilation and reconstruction was born the book that we offer, not without apprehension, to the enlightened public and to all friends of linguistics. (1959, pp. xiii–xv)

Saussure attempted to empirically analyze language, its construction, use, and parts. In fact, the theory addressed by Saussure has its roots in the notion of universal grammar. The relationship between Saussure's theory and the notion of universal grammar lies in the sense that the tradition of universal grammar was involved with the structuralist study of language. The major purpose of universal grammarians, during the seventeenth and eighteenth centuries, was not only a description of language but also its analysis that could offer general principles, which were considered pertinent to any language. One of the major differences between Saussure's theories and those of the universal grammarians is that, despite their recognition of speech as a relevant part of language, the grammarians did not address any study based on the phonetic structure of language. John Stoddart (1854) clarifies the purposes of universal grammar:

> Universal Grammar, on the contrary, disregarding that which is peculiar to the speech of this or that individual, tribe, nation, or race, considers only what is common to man [sic] in all ages and countries. . . . It is necessary to keep in view the distinction between Universal Grammar and Particular Grammar of different nations, ancient and modern. The word Grammar, taken in its comprehensive sense, may be briefly defined, the science of the relations of language considered as significant. . . . Universal Grammar is a science, Particular Grammar is an art; though like all other arts its foundations must be laid in science; and the science on which it rests is Universal Grammar. I am far from asserting that Universal Grammar has been hitherto so successfully cultivated, as to leave to future investigators no hope of improving this science. . . . Much, however, has been done. (pp. 20–21)

In fact, the tradition of universal grammar and the rational inquiry addressed by its grammarians assisted the development of structural linguistics during this century. Structural linguists are concerned with a factual and precise analysis of grammar. In other words, they are concerned with language as a formal system. Their study is focused on an accurate description and analysis of rules that compose structures of language as well as phonetic (sounds) and semantic (meanings) understandings of these structures. One of the most important representatives of structural linguistics in this century is Ferdinand de Saussure.

For Saussure, language is something that belongs to humankind. In his own words, "It is both a social product of the faculty of speech and a collection of necessary conventions that have been adopted by a social body to permit individuals to exercise that faculty" (1959, p. 9). Despite the recognition of the social aspect, Saussure does not understand these "necessary conventions" as necessary embodiments of ideologies. Furthermore, when he explains the meaning of language it is clear that he addresses a distinction between language (langue) and speech (parole). He argues that

> [i]n separating language from speaking we are at the same time separating: (1) what is social from what is individual; and (2) what is essential from what is accessory and more or less acci-

dental. Language is not a function of the speaker; it is a product that is passively assimilated by the individual. It never requires premeditation, and reflection enters in only for the purpose of classification. . . . Speaking, on the contrary, is an individual act. It is willful and intellectual. . . . Language, unlike speaking, is something that we can study separately. Although dead languages are no longer spoken, we can easily assimilate their linguistic organisms. We can dispense with the other elements of speech; indeed, the science of language is possible only if the other elements are excluded. Whereas speech is heterogeneous, language, as defined, is homogeneous. (1959, pp. 14–15)

Voloshinov (1973) explains that there exists a strong emphasis on an empirical understanding of language in linguistic science. He further asserts that this empirical understanding is connected to the idea of representing sounds (phonetics) rather than an understanding of language as an ideological sign. For Voloshinov, an understanding of language must go beyond a psycho-physiological analysis and beyond a phonetic and morphological analysis of language. For him, language cannot be merely placed within these categories. For this reason, Voloshinov situates Saussure as a representative of what he calls *abstract objectivism*. Contrary to a structuralist assumption about language, Voloshinov argues against the notion of universal grammar and challenges the objectivist notion that language is a mechanistic composition that can be internalized by individuals independent of social contexts. He reports that "if we claim that language as a system of incontestable and immutable norms exists objectively, we commit a gross error" (1973, p. 65). In order to understand Voloshinov's argument, it is necessary to clarify Saussure's analysis of language.

Contrary to Voloshinov and Bakhtin's perceptions, Saussure understands a sign as something psychological. From this understanding, Saussure addresses a distinction between signified (concept/idea) and signifier (what represents a concept—a word, for instance). Signified and signifier exist inside the concept of sign. Saussure (1959) writes:

The linguistic sign unites, not a thing and a name, but a concept and a sound-image. The latter is not the material sound, a purely physical thing, but the psychological imprint of the sound, the impression that it makes on our senses. The psychological character of our sound-images becomes apparent when we observe our own speech. Without moving our lips or tongue, we can talk to ourselves. . . . I propose to retain the word *sign* (signe) to designate the whole and to replace *concept* and *sound-image* respectively by *signified* (signifié) and *signifier* (signifiant); the last two terms have the advantage of indicating the opposition that separates them from each other and from the whole of which they are parts. [author's emphasis] (p. 67)

Furthermore, Saussure explains that the linguistic sign is arbitrary because there are many ways to represent a sign or, in his own words, a signified. He argues that a concept such as 'horse,' for instance, is not connected to the word *horse* because there are many ways to represent this concept, such as within diverse languages (e.g., 'horse' in English; 'cavalo' in Portuguese). However, a signifier is fixed within the community that uses it. For this reason, Saussure (1959) argues that "every means of expression used in society is based, in principle, on collective behavior or—what amounts to the same thing—on convention" (p. 68). In fact, Saussure establishes an analysis of parts of the sign—signifier and signified. What is interesting is that Saussure recognizes the influence exercised by social relations but he did not admit that these relations could represent vital aspects for his analysis of signs. Here, Voloshinov argues against the notion that a sign can be created and understood outside of social interaction or that words (ideological signs) can be studied outside of social-ideological interrelations. Voloshinov emphasizes that any sign is a material embodiment of ideology and, therefore, belongs to the social existence. Furthermore, any social phenomenon such as movements of the body, colors or sounds, for instance, functions as a sign. For this reason, the individual consciousness itself is completely filled with signs. Therefore, the understanding of a sign exists only within social interaction among individuals and their consciousness becomes consciousness only when consciousness has been filled with ideological content—the semiotic characteristic.

Since a word is a sign created within social interaction, Voloshinov disagrees with Saussure (1959) when the latter structuralist argues that "language, better than anything else, offers a basis for understanding the semiological problem; but language must, to put it correctly, be studied in itself; heretofore language has almost always been studied in connection with something else, from other viewpoints" (p. 16).

In fact, there exists a contradiction in Saussure's analysis of the sign. Saussure (1959) is emphatic when he argues that a semiotic study of signs belongs to psychology and that the role of linguists is to understand language as a system. However, he conceptualizes the meaning of sign by addressing the relevance of a semiotic approach to the sign. He explains that semiology should be the science to study the constitution of a sign and that linguistics should be part of semiology. Saussure (1959) asserts that

> *there is the viewpoint of the psychologist*, who studies the sign-mechanism in the individual . . . *but it does not lead beyond individual execution and does not reach the sign, which is social. . . . But to me the language problem is mainly semiological*, and all developments derive their significance from that important fact. *If we are to discover the true nature of language we must learn what it has in common with all semiological systems; linguistic forces that seem very important at first glance (e.g., the role of the vocal apparatus) will receive only secondary consideration. . . .* This procedure will do more than to clarify the linguistic problem. By studying rites, customs, etc. as signs, I believe that we shall throw new light on the facts and point up the need for including them in a science of semiology. [emphasis added] (p. 17)

It is worth noting that if Saussure (1959) views a sign as social and argues that language is, basically, a semiological problem, it appears that he could not, therefore, analyze a sign as psychological. However, the difference between Saussure's and Voloshinov's theories is that Saussure does not perceive the sign as socially mutable and changeable. In this sense, Saussure's analysis of the sign is limited because he perceive signs as "ready-made" codes.

Saussure (1959) argues that the two main aspects in the study of language are its synchronic and diachronic aspects. He explains that *synchronic linguistics* is concerned with the study of language as it is spoken and also the rules that govern its structures in speakers' minds. *Diachronic linguistics* analyzes the transformations of language within a successive substitution of terms in this language—changes that occur in time. The difference between synchronic and diachronic linguistics is that synchronic linguistics analyzes actual grammatical aspects of the language and the way in which they relate one with another, while diachronic linguistics analyzes the evolution of language. However, for Saussure, a synchronic understanding of language exists independently from a diachronic understanding. Again, Voloshinov (1973) assumes a completely different position and his critique is intense toward Saussure's assumptions.

A synchronic system, from the objective point of view, does not correspond to any real moment in the historical process of becoming. And indeed, to the historian of language, with his [or her] diachronic point of view, a synchronic system is not a real entity; it merely serves as a conventional scale on which to register the deviations occurring at every real instant in time. . . . We may suppose, for instance, that while Caesar was engaged in writing his works, the Latin language was for him a fixed, incontestable system of self-identical norms; but, for the historian of Latin, a continuous process of linguistic change was going on at the very moment that Caesar was working (whether or not the historian of Latin would be able to pinpoint those changes). (p. 66)

The problem for Voloshinov regarding Saussure's theory is that the synchronic aspect of language does not exist, even in an objective view, because this aspect exists only for a particular individual in a particular time. In fact, the divorce between synchrony and diachrony limits a broader understanding of language.

The major critique addressed by Voloshinov is that structuralist linguists do not consider the dynamic of the utterance (of speech performance) because the utterance as a social entity simply does not exist for them. Despite a sociological claim, Voloshinov (1973) argues that their tendency is an analysis of isolated aspects of language where historical changes are regarded as mere accidental transgressions. With respect to diachronic changes in language, Saussure (1959) notes that

if one speaks of law in synchrony, it is in the sense of an arrangement, a principle of regularity. Diachrony, on the contrary, supposes a dynamic force through which an effect is produced, a thing executed. But this imperative is not sufficient to warrant applying the concept of law to evolutionary facts; we can speak of law only when a set of facts obeys the same rule, and in spite of certain appearances to the contrary, diachronic events are always accidental and particular. The accidental and particular character of semantic facts is immediately apparent. That French poutre 'mare' has acquired the meaning 'piece of wood, rafter' is due to particular causes and does not depend on other changes that might have occurred at the same time. It is only one accident among all those registered in the history of language. (p. 93)

For Voloshinov (1973), this means that structuralist analysis consists in an abstract understanding of an utterance as a separate linguistic form. As he argues, the number of meanings of words varies according to the number of the contexts in which they are used. Therefore, the polysemantic aspect of a word cannot be ignored and advocates of abstract objectivism have a tendency to ignore multiple meanings, giving a definition for a word outside of its context. The issue here is that we never use a word without content and meaning. When a word is spoken it is inserted in an ideological context. Therefore, a linguistic form does not exist in itself but always within a process of understanding in which there exists an inter-exchange of the speaker's and listener's consciousness. In this sense, I agree with Voloshinov's critique of Saussure's analysis when he argues that the process of understanding is misunderstood as a mere recognition of linguistic forms.

## CONCLUSION

I believe the Marxian analysis of ideologies is crucial for understanding language because social interrelation among people is what guarantees the semiotic value of ideologies and, therefore, the very existence of language. In this sense, the Bakhtin circle offers an insightful analysis because its members recognize that these ideologies are the medium of our existence in relation to the world. Therefore, language as an ideological and mutable sign, shapes and constructs the way in which we perceive the world. This means if we are going to analyze language as a separate system, as Saussure suggested, we will lose the relevance of its existence. If we deny the assumption that language is a concrete ideological form, we will find no reason to utilize language in communication. If we are going to analyze a word in itself, we will see that words mean nothing unless they are placed in a social-ideological environment because the meaning of a word is always connected to the social location of an individual. It is the social location that will shape the ideological value (accents) of words.

When children go to school, they already possess a well-developed speaking consciousness, which is a consciousness built upon social interaction. Therefore, a student's consciousness is cultivated in a specific social context and words and utterances are inserted in specific meanings that are meaningful only for a particular social group. That is, meanings are permeated by a specific cultural understanding. When an individual is supposed to acquire a second language, numerous issues must be taken into account. Learning a second language, English for instance, does not mean an acquisition of vocabulary or a memorization of grammatical categories. For instance, in Portuguese, the words *mesa* (table), *cadeira* (chair), and *toalha* (towel) are feminine words, while *livro* (book) and *computador* (computer) are masculine words. A Portuguese as well as a Spanish speaker must learn that in English there are words that are neutral. This represents not only changes in the vocabulary or changes in the way in which words are classified but also changes in the way in which the *world* is classified or, in other words, changes in a speaker's consciousness. In this sense, some questions seem relevant for our analysis: What kind of curriculum has been valued by schools in terms of language learning and teaching? Have we considered the extraverbal contexts of utterances when we teach language? Have we considered language as a set of written standard rules outside of its context or have we considered language as an embodiment of ideologies in society? Have we considered language within a dynamic arena of oppositions or have we considered language as a static and incontestable form of expression? Have we taken into serious account that students have their own consciousness or have we tried to teach pseudo-empty minds the way in which they should understand language?

Language is, in itself, social because language would not exist if there were no social intercourses. The dialogic linguistic exchange, in which there occurs dynamic interrelations among people's consciousness, neither exists outside people's social context and their historical location, nor outside interpenetrating relationships with another's reactions or another's word. Following this perception, it is impossible to distinguish what is language and what is society when we use language. An understanding that language and society have a strong connection and inter-existence is crucial for the learning-teaching process of second language acquisition.

CHAPTER TWO

# THE HISTORICAL APPEAL

*The truth is not to be found in the golden*
*mean and is not a matter of compromise*
*between thesis and antithesis, but lies over*
*and beyond them, constituting a negation of*
*both thesis and antithesis alike.*
—Voloshinov (1973, p. 82)

If a conclusion exists about the purpose of bilingual education, it is
that there is no conclusion. As Courtney Cazden and Catherine Snow
(1990) point out, "'Bilingual education' is a seemingly simple label for a
complex phenomenon" (p. 9). Furthermore, Gary Cziko (1992) underscores the plethora of research in bilingual education when he argues that
"a search through the ERIC [Educational Resources Information Center]
computerized database found 921 bibliographic entries matching the
descriptors "bilingual education and program evaluation" or "bilingual
education and program effectiveness" from 1966 through September
1990" (p. 10).

The fact is assumptions about bilingual education surround our lives
and can be uncovered in the following questions: Why do some people
completely reject the idea of a bilingual program while others are ardent
advocates of such a program? What are the right ways to teach a second
language (L2)? What are immersion programs? What are the implications
for non-English-speaking students who are prohibited to speak in their
own language while they are in the classroom? Why are some bilingual
programs successful while others fail? Why it is necessary to have a bilin-

gual program? What are the levels of teachers' responsibility in a bilingual program? When does someone really know a second language?

Definitely, the label "bilingual education" has been used to refer to programs in which two languages are used in the classroom; to refer to programs in which bilingual students are enrolled; or to refer to programs in which non-English-speaking students must learn English as quickly as possible while their own language is neglected in the classrooms. Bilingual students are those who are considered members of language-minority groups "in a society that tends to identify bilingual children with educational risk" (Cazden and Snow, 1990, p. 9). It is indeed disturbingly ironic that in the United States bilingual students are considered to be at-risk. Not only does society itself reflect such an attitude but it also suggests monolingualism as an unsullied, unspoiled, uncontaminated essence.

The general public voice proclaims that teachers must teach for diversity and that the demographic changes demand this kind of teaching. For instance, Robert Barnes (1983) reports that in California during the spring of 1980 there were 325,748 students in kindergarten through grade twelve who should learn English as a second language and attend bilingual programs. According to the U.S. census of 1980, the majority of language-minority students were living in California, New York, Illinois, Texas, Florida, New Mexico, Arizona, Connecticut, and Hawaii. In 1986, for instance, there were 600,000 legal immigrants in the U.S.: 39 percent from Latin America and 44 percent from Asia. Sonia Nieto (1993) remarks that "one report estimates that there are currently between 1.2 million and 1.7 million such students [non-English speakers]. Even more dramatic is the expectation that by the year 2020, the number of children speaking a primary language other than English will be almost 6 million" (p. 196). Therefore, the demographic conditions reveal that the already significant number of non-English-speaking students (more than 50 percent in some school districts) will increase dramatically. The problem is U.S. schools are not prepared for such a demand, as Peter McLaren (1994a) explains:

> Although nearly 25 percent of all public school teachers in the United States had students with limited English proficiency (LEP) in their classes in 1980 and 1981, only 3.2 percent of those teachers said that they were equipped to deal with these students. (pp. 16–17)

Another problem is an explanation of the term *Limited English Proficient* (LEP), since school districts have diverse measures to classify the meaning of proficiency. As Alba Ambert and Sarah Melendez (1985) argue, "Language proficiency is a complex skill which cannot be adequately assessed using a single measure, at a given time, and under specific performance constraints" (p. 79). For instance, a student may read a text in a second language but have difficulty speaking this language. Another example includes the divergent ways of articulating a word in a second language, which can be considered as a lack of proficiency even if the student does not have any problems with writing the second language.

## BILINGUAL PROGRAMS

To clarify what is or at least what exists in terms of bilingual education, it is necessary to become familiar with a variety of types of bilingual instructional programs that have been practiced throughout the United States. Basically, there are five different bilingual instructional programs: *English As a Second Language* (ESL); *Transitional Bilingual Education* (TBE); *Maintenance* bilingual education; *Two-way Enrichment* (or developmental) bilingual education; and *Immersion* programs. Some of these programs have a subtractive outcome while others have an additive outcome. A subtractive outcome means the main goal is fluency in English without considering bilingualism as necessary. This is the case of TBE and Immersion programs. However, Maintenance and Two-way enrichment programs present an additive outcome since bilingualism is considered both academically and linguistically relevant. ESL programs provide English language instruction only, with little relation to the subject matter of the curriculum. The organization Teachers of English to Speakers of Other Languages (TESOL) endorses the aim that ESL is connected to the idea of acquiring a second language per se. Therefore, this program can also be considered subtractive despite the recognition that non-English speakers can use their language while learning English.

*English As a Second Language* is English language instruction out of regular classes. In other words, non-English-speaking students take special courses in English language instruction until they can be placed in regular content-area instructional classes. Usually, ESL programs are commonly used in schools where the population of non-English-speaking students includes a large variety of native languages other than English. In some schools, students have ESL classes for one period of the school day and also attend regular classes during other periods. In other schools, students spend one year in intensive ESL instruction before they can attend regular classes.

*Transitional Bilingual Education* consists of a transition from native to English language. In this program, non-English-speaking students receive instruction of content-areas in their own native language during a period of time (two or three years) and at the same time study the English language (in an ESL program). As soon as these students are considered proficient in English they are placed in regular classes with English-speaking students.

In *Maintenance* bilingual education, students receive instruction of content-areas in both their own native language and English, even when they are considered proficient in English. This means that non-English-speaking students do not have to leave the Maintenance bilingual program because it is expected that students can maintain proficiency in both languages. Furthermore, there exists a balance between the grading system of content-areas in English and in the students' own native language. The main goal in this program is that non-English-speaking students can become linguistically and academically bilingual.

*Two-way Enrichment* bilingual education is a program in which English-speaking students study another language while non-English-speaking students study English. Therefore, both groups—English-speaking and non-English-speaking students—are within the same situation of learning, that is, both groups are not bilingual but they can become bilingual. This program is possible in schools where numerous other languages do not exist. Usually, this program is used in schools where the non-English-speaking population is composed of Spanish speakers.

In *Immersion* programs, the instruction in all of the content-areas is taught in English. Usually, the students' proficiency level in English is considered and the instruction of content-areas is adapted according to this proficiency level. There is no specific time limit for students in this kind of program. Furthermore, this program is considered bilingual because students can use their native language in classrooms but all of the instruction is in English, including the teachers' responses.

## BILINGUAL EDUCATION WITHIN A PIECE OF HISTORY

Many political and social constituencies throughout the United States become heated when bilingual education is discussed. It seems the controversy surrounding bilingual education exists because what is being judged is not the importance of learning another language or the evaluation of bilingual programs, but rather which group is privileged with bilingual programs.

Many scholars have dedicated their work toward a complete historical understanding of bilingual education (e.g., Baker and Kanter, 1983; Stein, 1986; August and Garcia, 1988; Stewart, 1993). The major purpose of this section is not a complete historical overview but a discussion of some of the existing controversies between what is written in the laws and policies of bilingual education and the effects stemming from the political and social manipulation of these laws and policies. The following paragraphs represent just a few examples of this controversy.

The most important weapon of linguistic minorities in the United States was and is Title VI of the Civil Rights Act of 1964. Peter Kane (1967) notes that during the early 1960s

> [t]elevision news films of peaceful Negroes [*sic*] being abused, beaten, and arrested while they sat at a counter seeking service was nightly fare in living rooms across the nation. . . . Demonstrations [against African Americans] occurred in Nashville, Philadelphia, Chicago, and New York City as well as many other cities in both the South and North. In sum, in the centennial year of the Emancipation Proclamation the question of real freedom for the Negro [*sic*] had become America's foremost domestic issue. (pp. 30–31)

Therefore, there existed a public claim for legislative changes regarding these concerns. Consequently, new resolutions were introduced in the U.S. Congress. The new legislation—the Civil Rights Act—contained directives against segregation in public accommodations; against school segregation; and addressed equal voting rights. However, despite the fact that Title VI, as part of the Civil Rights Act, was approved to end the practice of segregation of the African-American people in schools, it also became a powerful way to establish bilingual programs.

> No person in the United States shall, on the ground of race, color or national origin, be excluded from participation in, be denied the benefits of, or be subjected to discrimination under any program or activity receiving Federal financial assistance. (U.S. Congressional Record, 1964, part 5, p. 645)

In other words, any program in which discrimination has been found to exist would not receive federal funds. Title VI recognizes that an individual should not be denied the opportunity of education—an exercise of human rights. Consequently, an understanding of the necessity of special instruction for non-English-speaking students began. In fact, Title VI should represent protection for language-minority students with respect to their educational achievement and it should also ensure equal educational opportunity to any language-minority students. However, the reality was controversial.

In 1966, Anne Stemmler participated in one of the first educational research projects dealing with the language development and reading skills of Spanish-speaking children in Texas. In Texas, at that time, it was estimated that out of 100,000 non-English-speaking students, more than 50 percent would have dropped out of school by the end of their elementary years. In a preliminary stage of her research, Stemmler (1966) writes:

> For the educationally disadvantaged Spanish-speaking child, there are painfully few parallels between critical aspects of the foregoing band required for reading and his experiences and behaviors. . . . His [or her] whole language development in Spanish is discarded. Because of his environment, many of his [or her] experiences are often judged irrelevant for academic learning and reading. For example, the currently used readiness programs often depict experiences remote from those of this child. The disadvantagedness also lessens the probability of his [or her] having developed the needed perceptual and cognitive behaviors related to reading. In a very real sense, the child is experiencing rejection in many areas of his [or her] development. (p. 51)

Not only were their experiences considered irrelevant but non-English-speaking students were also considered to be mentally retarded. Colman Stein (1986) argues that, during the 1960s and even during the 1970s, non-English-speaking students were placed in Educable Mentally Retarded (EMR) classes because their IQ scores were low. However, since IQ tests were written in English, these non-English-speaking students were considered deficient learners because their linguistic performance in English was directly connected to levels of intelligence. One question seems appropriate: After Stemmler's (1966) preliminary conclusions, what changed in bilingual education?

Despite the strong weapon against discrimination after Title VI in 1964, non-English-speaking students had their rights protected by the Supreme Court's Lau v. Nichols (Kinney Kinmon Lau v. Alan Nichols). David Stewart (1993) clarifies that Lau v. Nichols was the result of Chinese students' actions against the San Francisco school system because this district was not providing adequate instruction. This Chinese group rejected the educational discrimination facing them, arguing that there was a violation of Title VI, because English was the language mandated by California. Furthermore, these students were forced to demonstrate proficiency in English as a prerequisite to high school; and all classes were taught in English. Almost 1,800 Chinese students were not receiving adequate education and were being discriminated against because they did not know English. That is, these students were not within the equal educational opportunity addressed by Title VI, because all school instruction was undertaken in English. Therefore, in 1974, The Supreme Court declared:

> [January 21, 1974] Moreover §8573 of the Education Code provides that no pupil shall receive a diploma of graduation from grade 12 who has not met the standards of proficiency in "English," as well as other prescribed subjects. Moreover by §12101 of the Education Code children between the ages of six and 16 years are (with exceptions not material here) "subject to compulsory full-time education." Under these state imposed standards *there is no equality of treatment merely by providing students with the same facilities, textbooks, teachers, and curriculum*; for students who do not understand English are effectively foreclosed from any meaningful education. Basic English skills are at the very core of what these public schools teach. Imposition of a requirement that, before a child can effectively participate in the educational program, he must already have acquired those basic skills is to make a mockery of public education. *We know that those who do not understand English are certain to find their classroom experiences wholly incomprehensible and in no way meaningful.* We do not reach the Equal Protection Clause argument which has been advanced but rely solely on §601 of the Civil

Rights Act of 1964. . . . That section bans discrimination based "on the ground of race, color, or national origin," in "any program or activity receiving federal financial assistance." The school district involved in this litigation receives large amounts of federal financial assistance. [emphasis added] (Baker and Kanter, 1983, p. 206)

Another relevant aspect of the Lau decision was that federal legislation extended the Lau conclusions to all public school districts. After Lau v. Nichols (or Lau Remedies), a myriad of new Court decisions mandated changes in school programs where non-English-speaking students were enrolled, such as Aspira of New York, Inc. v. Board of Education of the city of New York, 1974 (182,000 Spanish-speaking students in New York City were not demonstrating academic improvement because they could not understand English); Arroyo v. Barbarito, 1975 (2,295 Puerto Rican students in the New Haven public school system complained against the educational programs that neglected their linguistic needs); and Rios v. Read, 1977 (questioned the effectiveness of ESL programs offered by Patchogue-Medford school district in Long Island since students did not demonstrate academic progress and fluency in English). All of these Court decisions were based on the violation of the Lau decision which, therefore, represented a beginning in the implementation of policies to protect the rights of language minorities.

In her historical research about education of Mexican Americans, Guadalupe San Miguel Jr. (1987) addresses the controversy surrounding bilingual education when she says that, some time ago, Mexican Americans could study in public schools, but they were forced to study in already segregated African-American and Indian-American schools. She also asserts that, at the present time, the segregation faced by Mexican Americans is not constitutional or based on state statutes; rather, this segregation is based on school board regulations and educational practices. But according to Arizona's Constitution, for instance, segregation goes beyond the ideological movement that has permeated United Statians' minds during the last twenty years or more, because this ideology of segregation, when put into law, officially becomes legitimated by the state. This ideology was embodied, for instance, in Proposition 106 of Arizona's Constitution.

Section 1. English As the Official Language; Applicability
   (1) The English language is the official language of the
      State of Arizona.
   (2) As the official language of this State, the English lan-
      guage is the language of the ballot, the public schools,
      and all government functions and actions.
Section 2. Requiring This State to Preserve, Protect, and
   Enhance English. This State and all political subdivisions of
   this State shall take all reasonable steps to preserve, protect
   and enhance the role of the English language as the sole official language of the State of Arizona.
Section 3. Prohibiting This State from Using or Requiring the
   Use of Languages Other Than English; Exceptions . . . (2)
   This State and all political subdivisions of this State may act
   in a language other than English under any of the following
   circumstances:
         (a) to assist students who are not proficient in the
            English language, to the extent necessary to com-
            ply with federal law, by giving educational instruc-
            tion in a language other than English to provide as
            rapid as possible a transition to English;
         (b) to comply with other federal laws;
         (c) to teach a student a foreign language as part of a
            required or voluntary educational curriculum.
   (Amended Article XXVIII of Arizona's Constitution, 1988,
   p. 35)

In fact, the assumptions addressed by supporters of English as the official
language (English-only movement) consist of political conflicts connected
to social and economical constraints rather than a discussion of language
itself. By way of illustration, many of the immigrants who live today in the
United States are a product of the transference of Latin American lands to
the United States many years ago; a product of the Cuban Revolution in
1959, which resulted in an enormous influx of upper-class Cuban refugees
to Florida; and a product of the wars for which the United States was at
least partially responsible. The dominant United States perspective
absolves U.S. participation in foreign wars because it is perceived by many
United Statians that the politics of the United States are designed to assist

other countries economically and in becoming more democratic. Therefore, the dominant U.S. ideology is that refugees and immigrants must be responsible to learn English as quickly as possible.

David Stewart (1993) argues that, in the last twenty years, the United States has admitted more refugees than any other country. He also explains that the refugees' acceptance is determined by the U.S. Congress, and in 1991 the ceiling on refugees was 131,000 but this number would increase to 480,000 by the end of 1995. However, "The Immigration and Naturalization Service (INS) has been accused by immigrant advocate groups of harassment, or even abuse and brutality" (Stewart, 1993, p. 35). In fact, immigrants face a confusing situation because once they become permanent residents, they may not vote and are prohibited to hold certain categories of governmental jobs. For instance, Martin Marger (1994) argues that

> Mexican Americans have maintained a notoriously low rate of political participation. . . . Several factors may account for this. First, and perhaps most important, a large percentage of Mexican Americans are poor [and] lower-income people in general display lower rates of political activity. . . . Finally, in the Southwest, tactics designed to prevent Mexican Americans from voting, such as the poll tax, gerrymandering of ethnic districts, literacy tests, intimidation, and even violence. . . . Low political participation and discriminatory practices have resulted in serious political underrepresentation at local and state levels. In Los Angeles, for example, with the largest Mexican-American community in the country, only two Chicanos sit on the fifteen-member city council. (p. 308)

Therefore, the ideology of discrimination and segregation seems an ideology that has been cultivated by the U.S. government, including the manufactured illusion that being a permanent resident is being a citizen. Furthermore, information is constantly distorted and a large part of the U.S. population has distorted answers and reactions. Donaldo Macedo (1993) provides one example of this distortion.

> The selective selection of our strong support for human rights becomes glaringly clear in the case of Haitians. In fact, the *Boston Globe*, confident of readers' inability to link historical events, published a front page article on the U.S. Supreme

Court decision that allowed the administration to repatriate thousands of Haitian refugees. On page 2 of the same issue, the *Globe* also ran a story about groups organized in Miami to search for and assist Cuban boat people to reach their final destination in Florida. It is this lack of connectedness that helped Bush to prevail in erasing our historical memory file on foreign policy in order to garner support for his fabricated high-tech war in the Gulf. . . . This fragmentation serves to create a self-serving history that feeds the recontextualization of a distorted and often false reality, leading (sometimes) to a specialization of barbarism ipso facto. (p. 194)

Many people in the United States continue to believe that U.S. students do not need to learn a second language. Usually, a foreign language can be taught in U.S. colleges or even in high schools but this is not usually a requirement. This is also true for many academic programs at universities, including many doctoral programs. The result is that the large majority of U.S. students are monolingual, as Richard Lambert (1994) notes:

> [M]ost students in Europe do study second and third languages, often at the same time, and issues of language choice in European foreign language plans are often quite specific concerning how these multiple tracks should be orchestrated. We in the United States, however, pay very little direct attention to multiple foreign language learning . . . [and] we have no tradition of facilitating multiple language learning or even paying attention to it. . . . Until adults in our society both value and use foreign language skills, language teaching in school will continue to be viewed as marginal by both students and school administrators. (pp. 54–56)

In fact, the sense that U.S. people can be happily monolingual lies in the perspective of international economic and political enterprise among countries. International U.S. domination and imperialism have been translated into a hegemonic understanding that if people want to succeed professionally they have to know U.S. English. As Judith Lessow-Hurley (1991) remarks, "All over the world, knowledge of English is considered essential" (p. 67). This message is present, for instance, in most countries of Latin America, which follow a national curriculum that maintains the assumption that students have to learn U.S. English during middle and high school. Another example in Latin America is that, in Brazil, dissertation abstracts at masters or doctoral levels must be written in English and graduate students must submit to second language tests.

Some of the initiatives in U.S. schools regarding second language acquisition by United Statians have been related to world market relations. As Carol Fixman (1990) notes,

> as a firm increases its business in developing countries, it will find that knowledge of English is less widespread in the local populations. Thus it will become more important for company employees to know the local languages. . . . Countries that were named as particularly difficult for conducting business in English include Japan, Korea, China, and the Soviet Union. . . . English skills are not very common there. In all of these areas, U.S. companies appear to have a greater need to have access to skills in the local languages. (p. 29)

For instance, Sarah Moore (1994) mentions the Geraldine Dodge Chinese Initiative which, in 1982, chose seven metropolitan areas for the development of Chinese high school language programs to which Chinese teachers were imported "to provide fresh perspectives" (p. 85) about China. Another example addressed by Moore (1994) is the Ford Foundation Program for Russian, which, like the Geraldine Dodge Chinese Initiative, imported teachers from Russia "who spent one year serving as resource" (p. 86) in U.S. high schools. On the other hand, Frederick Starr (1994) emphasizes that despite these few initiatives, national policies are reinforcing the lack of second language training for United Statians. He argues that

> American corporations opted for English for intrafirm communication, relegating foreign language use mainly to low-level contacts with clients and suppliers. Thanks to this, demand for foreign language competency in the corporate world is modest, with partial exception of those firms dealing with Japan. Even in this case, most American firms prefer to hire foreign nationals rather than provide language training for Americans. . . . Moreover, granted that more firms will engage in foreign trade in the future, even as positive a development as the North American Free Trade Agreement [NAFTA] will do more to

stimulate the study of English in Mexico than of Spanish in the United States and Canada. (p. 144)

*The New York Times*, arguably the most influential newspaper in the United States, usually has sharp words against bilingual programs. Ricardo Otheguy (1991) writes that "*The New York Times . . .* regularly rails against expensive bilingual education programs that never work, a fact, its editors argue, that accords with every known pedagogical theory and with common sense" (p. 410). As acceptance of languages means acceptance of diverse cultures, U.S. autonomy and nationalism is often seen as vulnerable with respect to the demands made by cultural diversity. Therefore, the history of non-English-speaking people in the United States has been one of political and educational suffering, even after the appearance of Title VII.

Title VII is the *Bilingual Education Act*, which was approved and signed by President Lyndon Johnson in 1968. The Act designed "local grantees to maintain programs of bilingual education when federal funding is reduced or no longer available" (Baker and Kanter, 1983, p. xiii). Therefore, in 1968, the need for bilingual education could no longer be perceived as simply isolated protests in diverse school districts because it became, for the first time, a federal policy.

The Bilingual Education Act (Title VII) was an amendment to the Elementary and Secondary Education Act. This amendment was addressed by Senator Ralph Yarborough (D) because, at that time in Texas, there were alarmingly high dropout rates of non-English-speaking students (Spanish speakers). In fact, the Bilingual Education Act was the consequence of social and political pressure stemming from the results of the National Education Association (NEA) report in 1966, which characterized the depressing treatment of non-English-speaking students in U.S. schools. Senator Yarborough confidently defended his ideas in the Congress:

Imagine the situation that confronts a certain youngster in my part of the country. A youngster spends his [or her] formative years in a warm, friendly environment of his [or her] family and friends—an environment in which Spanish is spoken. At age 5 or 6 he [or she] is taken to school. What a profound shock he [or she] encounters the first day there, where he [or she] is made to know in no uncertain terms that he [or she] may speak no Spanish at school. He [or she] must speak English, a language which he [or she] scarcely knows, both in the classroom and on the playground. If he [or she] is caught speaking Spanish, he [or she] will be punished. (Secada, 1990, p. 88)

While Title VII represented a positive gain for non-English-speaking students, especially Spanish-speaking students, it also represented possibilities for Yarborough's reelection. Title VII was a powerful decision to enhance the improvement of teacher training as well as the development of bilingual instructional materials and their maintenance. For instance, in 1969, the Title VII program received $7.5 million distributed among seventy-six projects.

Gary Cziko (1992) mentions one of the most famous evaluations of bilingual education in the United States during the 1970s. Cziko (1992) explains that this evaluation, promoted by the American Institute of Research (AIR), analyzed the influence of Title VII bilingual programs. As Cziko (1992) attests, during the 1970s the evaluation promoted by the AIR analyzed 11,500 students' performances (from grades two through six). This evaluation consisted of a measurement of oral and written comprehension as well as mathematics in both English and Spanish. The final conclusion was that Title VII had no consistent impact on students' achievement in learning a L2 (English). Cziko (1992) criticizes the AIR evaluation, saying that "the report provides no guidance on how lesser quality bilingual programs could be improved" (p. 11). In other words, the AIR evaluation did not address any recommendation of investigating different methods of teaching-learning in bilingual education.

Title VII is restricted to Transitional Bilingual Education programs but advocates of TBE programs affirm that funds are never sufficient to reach a significant number of students who have little or no proficiency in English (Epstein, 1977). During the 1970s, it was estimated that TBE programs would need $2 billion to reach 3.6 million students. Therefore, the TBE advocates believe this is the reason for the AIR impact and its terrible results. Furthermore, an analysis of the AIR evaluation was promoted by the Intercultural Development Research Association (IDRA), which identified enormous amounts of discrepancies. Among many problems, it was found out that only 26 percent of the teachers who participated in the AIR evaluation had the appropriate credentials to teach in a bilingual program; one-third of the non-Title VII teachers were involved in TBE programs; 49.6 percent of the teachers admitted they did not know any other language but English; and differences among school districts (e.g., organization, methodologies, teacher training and qualifications) were not taken into account (Cardenas, 1977).

The social and political implications of the AIR evaluation were dangerous because the evaluation represented negative propaganda that the government was funding bilingual programs, which had no impact on students' achievement in learning a second language (English). However, as the above explanations illustrate, there was a manipulative result that, undoubtedly, reached United Statians' minds—that bilingual education was a waste of time and public money. For this reason, The Bilingual Education Act (Title VII) has an interesting history of authorizations and reauthorizations.

A reauthorization of any law means that the Congress stipulates the level of the law's authorization. In other words, the amount of federal funding available each year is stipulated and if there is no reauthorization, programs that depend on federal funding cease to exist. However, the level of authorization has not been received by bilingual programs in its complete request. For instance, in 1985, during the Reagan administration, "Bilingual education had a $176 million authorization level, but only received $143 million" (Stein, 1986, p. 171). The incontestable fact is that, in order to prevail, Title VII needs federal funding and history indicates that the U.S. administration has had divergent positions regarding the maintenance of bilingual education.

David Stewart (1993) argues that despite the fact that the Bilingual Education Act (Title VII) was reauthorized by President Richard Nixon, the Title presented a myriad of changes from the first bill introduced by Yarborough. Stewart (1993) writes:

> one of these [differences] was that the target group was changed from 'Spanish-speaking children' to 'children of limited English-speaking ability'. From the perspective of some bilingual education advocates, this broadening of focus was not entirely desirable in that it emphasized the concept of deficiency in the English language rather than proficiency in another language. Strengthening of the native language was not included. (p. 157)

After changes, Title VII was not limited to Spanish-speaking students as Yarborough first suggested. Then, in 1974, Title VII was reauthorized with more changes. At this time, the difference was that the students' native language was encouraged within existing methodologies by all public school districts. Another difference was that the cultural heritage of non-English-speaking students was emphasized in schools and that bilingual education would receive $58.4 million in federal funding. However, despite the apparent support of the Nixon administration, there still existed some problems with bilingual education. For instance, it was during the Nixon administration that many teachers were hired without any kind of bilingual education qualifications.

A new reauthorization in the Bilingual Education Act occurred during President Jimmy Carter's administration. In 1978, the Congress allowed the utilization of languages other than English in classrooms but only to guarantee success in the transition from the other language to English. For this reason, the Carter administration maintained Title VII only for the purposes of Transitional Bilingual Education programs. Furthermore, bilingual education was made available for all students independently of socio-economic levels. While on the one hand, the reality of this bilingual consent was implicit within a message of election needs during 1980, when the Carter administration needed a large number of votes among Hispanics in Texas, California, and New York (Stein, 1986), on the other hand, programs such as the Maintenance bilingual education were not even considered.

Joseph Califano, Carter's Secretary of the Department of Health, Education and Welfare (HEW) defended the Title VII program since its first introduction in 1968. However, in 1978, Califano drastically changed his position and questioned bilingual education based on Carter's assumption that schools should teach only English. Colman Stein (1986) summarizes:

> The Ford and Carter administrations were less than enthusiastic about bilingual education. Congress and few federal officials like Commissioner Bell and Vice-President Mondale sustained it, but no clear policy direction emerged. The program floated in a sea of ambiguity. (p. 41)

Terrel Bell had been Commissioner of Education during the Ford administration. Later, Bell was appointed as Secretary of Education when Ronald Reagan began his presidency. Despite Bell's appeal to old-fashioned excellence in U.S. schools, he addressed the necessity of bilingual education to help minorities since the beginning of his appointment. However, in 1984, Bell left the government and William Bennett replaced him as the new Secretary of Education—the nightmare for language minorities was just beginning.

Ronald Reagan's government is seriously accused of a lack of respect for non-English speakers in schools. Ricardo Otheguy (1991) notes that, during the Reagan administration, federal regulations for bilingual programs were annulled. Furthermore, Sonia Nieto (1993) states that when questioned about bilingual education, President Reagan answered with the following words: "It is absolutely wrong and against American concept to have a bilingual education program that is now openly, admittedly dedicated to preserving their native language and never getting them adequate in English so they can go out into the job market" (p. 200). Joe Kincheloe summarizes Reagan's ideal and the distorted social reasoning of this ideal.

> Part of the mythology that the right-wing has created to sustain its power involves the portrayal of a golden age of American education. It was a 'simpler, more natural time' when students behaved, the basics were taught, and teachers were dedicated to their noble profession. Ronald Reagan built a career on creating nostalgia for this golden age. If we would just get prayer back in the school, restore discipline like Joe Clark did in New Jersey, and teach reverence for American traditions, we could refind our lost glory. . . . Reagan and his educational reformers erased our 'dangerous memories.' Vietnam became our finest hour in defense of freedom, and the quest for social and racial justice became the clammering of the special interests. William Bennett warned against using social studies to teach about racial issues; instead, he argued, we should be teaching the 'great facts' of American history. (Steinberg, 1992, p. 401)

It is a fact that during the Reagan administration, William Bennett, the Secretary of Education, was the worst enemy bilingual programs in the United States had ever confronted. For instance, federal funding under the Bilingual Education Act (Title VII) was reduced by 47 percent between 1980 and 1988. However, despite the Reagan administration as a strong opponent, it was in 1988 that the Bilingual Education Act was reauthorized with more flexibility than ever. David Stewart (1993) explains that "it was decided to allow 25 percent of the funds for ESL and other English-based methods" (p. 160). This means that the new reauthorization represented a larger room for bilingual programs other than just the Transitional Bilingual Education program. On the other hand, James

Lyons (1990) argues that the Reagan administration was not actively involved in the 1988 flexible reauthorization. He explains that Senator Edward Kennedy, chairman of the Labor and Human Resources Committee, was a strong advocate of this new reauthorization. Kennedy defended his ideas in the Congress with the following words:

> This enhanced funding flexibility should be exercised in a responsible fashion, and I urge both the Department of Education and my colleagues on the Senate and House Appropriations Committees to allocate nonreserved funds to those Part A programs which, on the basis of objective program evaluation and research data, are shown to be most effective in helping limited-English-proficient students achieve academic success. In this regard, I am troubled by the fact that the Department of Education currently provide only two grants, amounting to less than one-quarter of all Part A funds, for two-way developmental bilingual education programs. Locally funded two-way bilingual education programs have proven effective in meeting the second language learning needs of both limited-English-proficient students and monolingual-English students in a positive, integrated educational environment. . . . Programs like these deserve additional Federal support. (Lyons, 1990, p. 77)

The fact is Title VII did not provide the necessary funds for bilingual education programs around the country despite the strong reactions of probilingual education organizations such as the National Association for Bilingual Education (NABE) and the National Council of La Raza (NCLR), which provide information regarding policy analysis; suggest parameters for reauthorizations; and specify the needs of bilingual programs. It is also a fact that, during the Reagan administration, Title VII provided for only 10 percent of more than 3.7 million students considered Limited English Proficient who should have received bilingual education. Furthermore, the way in which federal funds were distributed among U.S. states was completely unequal and inappropriate, as Colman Stein (1986) notes:

> As many local districts receive greater numbers of LEP students, they try to find ways to get larger chunks of Title VII money. Some put themselves through contortions to better

qualify for these funds. New York City, for example, began competing for federal funds not as one local district, but as 32 community school districts. . . . But they are not fully autonomous—there is still one local education agency. Using the community district approach, over 80 percent of them received Title VII funds. The city as a whole received half as much Title VII money as the entire state of California, which has many more LEP students. New York City (114,000 LEP students) outpaced Los Angeles (143,000 LEP students) $7.2 million to $338,000 in Title VII funds in a recent year. (p. 173)

Beyond the unfair competition among the U.S. states there historically existed the pressure of Reagan's administration, during 1981, to place Title VII into the Chapter 2 block grant, which would mean single authorization of local funds instead of the federal level. However, this attempt was not realized due to the protests of the Congressional Hispanic Caucus, which argued that local funds would not guarantee the maintenance of bilingual education (August and Garcia, 1988).

The facts surrounding bilingual education during George Bush's era are not divergent from Reagan's. Within the goals to be achieved by the year 2000, Bush's Department of Education did not mention the relevance of knowing languages other than English. This is especially noted, for instance, in the following part of the goals:

American students will leave grades four, eight, and twelve having demonstrated competency in challenging subject matter including English, mathematics, science, history and geography; and every school in America will ensure that all students learn to use their minds well, so they may be prepared for responsible citizenship, further learning, and productive employment in our modern economy." (United States Department of Education. *The Condition of Bilingual Education in the Nation: A Report to the Congress and the President*, 1991, p. 4)

According to the Department of Education, in the school year 1989–1990 there existed 2.2 million Limited English Proficient students. The Department, in its 1991 report, argues that the major problem faced by bilingual education programs is an inconsistency of identifying the meaning of LEP students. In other words, the Department of Education recognizes that states and school districts have a variety of standards to classify, identify, and evaluate LEP students.

Keeping in mind that bilingual education has to be strongly associated with the idea of helping minorities become literate citizens, during Reagan's and Bush's administration Title VII was reauthorized and received federal funds not only to maintain existing programs but also to elaborate a major longitudinal study developed by David Ramirez, whose final report was completed in February 1991.

David Ramirez's longitudinal study was developed over an eight-year-period, beginning in fiscal year 1983–1984 and ending in fiscal year 1990–1991. According to Ramirez's (1991) final report, all teachers were bilingual and 2,000 LEP students from California, Florida, New Jersey, New York, and Texas participated in the study. The study tested three programs: Immersion; Early-exit (thirty to sixty minutes a day with native language instruction during three years); and Late-exit (40 percent of the school day with substantial instruction in native language during six years). These three programs have the identical goal of acquiring English language skills towards an English-only classroom. The results demonstrate that when LEP students are provided with an ample amount of their primary language in classes—a Late-exit program—they have a major potentiality to succeed in English-only classrooms. However, Ramirez (1991) emphasizes that the process of acquiring English skills takes at least six years—which represents a very important aspect for bilingual education and its policies.

With the final results of the presidential election in 1992, the United States has a Democratic president after many years of Republican domination. President Bill Clinton seems supportive of bilingual education; he appointed Eugene Garcia, a professor at the University of California (Santa Barbara) who is dedicated to bilingual education within a multicultural view, as the Director of the Office of Bilingual Education and Minority Language Affairs in the U.S. Department of Education.

In an interview with Peter McLaren (1994b), Eugene Garcia explains his position in the face of bilingual education when questioned about his own philosophy of education.

> We have to make sure that we communicate to the broader population the importance of biliteracy and multiculturalism and of changing the educational agenda. . . . And to make sure that the broader population recognizes and acknowledges the important human resource this population provides . . . it is an agenda that

includes bilingualism and biliteracy; it's an additive model; that's my initial agenda—a new vision. . . . This is my personal philosophy—everyone should be bilingual and have a multicultural consciousness and awareness; we'll be better people if we have multiple perspectives and languages. . . . In the context of my federal position, my personal philosophy will definitely be the basis, serve as part of my own analysis for what might be appropriate. But, of course, my philosophy won't be the sole basis. There are federal laws, the role of the federal government, other issues than my personal philosophy. (p. 76)

Nevertheless, the Clinton administration needs to face the fact that all of the political aspects that followed in the wake of the first appearance of Title VII have been echoed in bilingual education debates for more than a decade. On the one hand, there are advocates of bilingual programs in which non-English speakers are encouraged to learn subject matters through their own language and are slowly introduced to English as L2— *English-plus*. On the other hand, there are advocates of immersion or submersion programs that reinforce English learning while avoiding Spanish or other non-English languages in classrooms. In this sense, students are supposed to achieve a transition from their native language into English as fast as possible—*English-only*.

At the present time, Title VII funds are used for basic instructional programs, research, graduate education (for students who are proficient in English and Spanish), and materials for use in bilingual classrooms. However, the position of Title VII is always threatened because of this extensive debate—English-only versus English-plus—which goes beyond the discussion of second language acquisition itself.

The political impact of the English-only movement has been considerably strong, especially because policy makers question the security of U.S. nationalism. On this note, Ofelia García and Ricardo Otheguy (1994) write:

As the multilingual world turns, little change seems apparent in the national sociolinguistic paradigm of the United States, where English monolingualism continues to be seen as a mark of power and prestige . . . we would need to alter a national posture that almost always in fact, if only occasionally in name, is inspired by an English-only ideology. (p. 119)

This movement advocates that language minorities can be successful as economically progressive citizens only if they can understand and accept the importance of cultural assimilation. Hence, for some congresspeople, U.S. nationalism represents the protection of English as the only official and tolerable language. For instance, in 1981, Senator Hayakawa (R) proposed the *English Language Amendment* (ELA), which declares that English should be the official language in the United States. Nancy Hornberger (1990) reports that since 1981 this amendment has been constantly introduced at the beginning of each two-year congressional session. Hornberger (1990) explains that

> The English Plus Information Clearinghouse reports that 13 states defeated such legislation in 1987, 4 in 1988, and 3 in 1989, but Alabama, Arkansas, California, Georgia, Illinois, Indiana, Kentucky, Mississippi, Nebraska, North Carolina, North Dakota, Ohio, South Carolina, Tennessee, and Virginia have all passed some kind of English-as-official-language legislation—resolution, statute, or constitutional amendment. (p. 15)

Furthermore, it was during the Reagan and Bush administrations that the English-only movement was at its most influential, ever since Title VII was first authorized, because these administrations supported the idea that immigrant children should be taught English through an "accelerated" methodology of transition for "their own good." This assumption hides the fact that conservative congresspeople advocate a monolingual society through a xenophobic understanding of national protection. Peter McLaren questions this conservative notion of nationalism when he argues:

> What kind of citizens do these conservative educators want produced by the schools? I think it's quite obvious that they want citizens who are committed to entrepreneurship, who will fight to keep English the official language of the country, who give lip service to democracy while really advocating a consumer culture who will cherish and defend neocolonial imperatives of a new world order ruled by the United States. (Steinberg, 1992, p. 403)

The fact that the English-only movement is a form of ethnic suppression cannot be denied. Historically, dominant U.S. groups desire immigrant labor but reject the social struggle that these immigrants have to face. This means that immigrants' ethnic diversity must be largely erased since it represents a threat to the old cultural conservatism of the "American dream"—a dream that does not belong to other groups of North, Central, and South 'Americans'. Therefore, supporters of the English-only movement advocate that bilingual education is counterproductive for language minorities and that if the United States provides bilingual education, non-English-speaking students should not spend more than three years in TBE programs. For instance, Mary McGroarty (1992) explains the demographics of the English-only movement—a movement that basically approves and supports Hayakawa's English Language Amendment.

> The English-only movement represents not the official stance of any elected government body in the United States but a coalition of private lobbying groups with a strong nativist strain. . . . One group is the 100,000-member *English First*, of Springfield, Va. The other, *U.S. English*, with 240,000 members, was established in 1983. . . . These two groups provide the ideological and financial support for national and local legislation to make English official and restrict use of other languages. [emphasis added] (p. 8)

In addition, McGroarty (1992) elucidates that these two groups are not alone on this issue. There are other lobbying groups that equally support ELA, such as the National Grange, the American Legion, and the Polish American Congress. These groups defend the idea that the acceptance of diverse languages produces fragmentation in U.S. society.

Gary Imhoff (1990) writes about *U.S. English*, a nonprofit public-interest organization that is "committed to promoting the use of English in the political, economic, and intellectual life of the nation" (p. 49). Imhoff (1990) argues that *U.S. English* advocates believe that claims for bilingual education stemmed from Hispanic organizations that reinforce separatism instead of an emphasis on the commonalties and integration of groups and "subgroups" (p. 48). The following principles are addressed by *U.S. English*:

> In a pluralistic society such as ours, government should foster the similarities that unite us rather than the differences that separate us. The nation's public schools have a special responsibility to help students who do not speak English to learn the language as quickly as possible. Quality teaching of English should be part of every student's curriculum, at every academic level. . . .

All candidates for U.S. citizenship should be required to demonstrate the ability to understand, speak, read, and write simple English [*What is simple English?*] and demonstrate basic understanding of our system of government. [emphasis/comment added] (Imhoff, 1990, p. 49)

In fact, *U.S. English* advocates believe that if bilingual education is understood under the assumption that foreign languages must be considered for the purposes of instruction, this represents a threat to the defense of the U.S. common language. Furthermore, they argue that bilingual education has not improved students' achievement in standardized tests even after twenty years of research and federal funds. Imhoff (1990), a *U.S. English* consultant, writes that "U.S. English has attempted to center the bilingual-education debate on what is in the best interests of the non-English-speaking children" (p. 61). However, the attempt of *U.S. English* means acculturation in which diverse ethnic identities must be erased toward a commonsensical understanding that cultural pluralism means marginality. In this sense, I agree with Raul Yzaguirre, president of the National Council of La Raza, who says that "U.S. English is to Hispanics as the Ku Klux Klan is to blacks [*sic*]" (Imhoff, 1990, p. 49).

Contrary to the English-only movement, the English-plus movement supports the rights of individuals to use other languages. For the purposes of this movement, there exists a coalition of professional groups that represent language teachers, such as the American Council on the Teaching of Foreign Languages; the National Council of Teachers of English; and Teachers of English to Speakers of Other Languages. These groups have been united since 1988 toward a public understanding that language freedom is not a threat to the nation and the officialization of English is counterproductive. This movement was created due to the actions of the National Immigration, Refugee, and Citizenship Forum—a civil rights group—and the Joint National Committee on Languages (McGroarty, 1992).

Courtney Cazden and Catherine Snow (1990), English-plus advocates, argue that bilingual education cannot only be understood as the use of Spanish in public schools but also the use of any several diverse languages including those of "indigenous and immigrant groups" (p. 9). Therefore, cultural plurality is a relevant issue for English-plus advocates because they understand monolingualism as a negative educational outcome. For instance, Arturo Madrid (1990), who worked as Director of the

Fund for the Improvement of Postsecondary Education, U.S. Department of Education, argues that the defense of official English addressed by representatives of the English-only movement is insane. He remarks that

> [m]aking English the official language of the United States is a false policy issue. . . . *Language policy has been an instrument of control, used to exclude certain groups from participating fully in America's institutions as well as to deny them the rights and benefits that accrue to members of this nation.* The most pernicious historical example of this was the de jure and de facto denial of English-language literacy to American Indians as well as to the population of African and Mexican origins. . . . *Contrary to popular belief, American society never enjoyed a golden age in which we all spoke English; we never were all one linguistically. The history of the United States is one of bi- and multi-lingualism.* At the time of the Declaration of Independence, for example, a significant proportion of the population spoke German. . . . No mention of language choice, for instance, is made in the Declaration of Independence or in the United States Constitution. Far more important as forces to unify the nation were individual rights, freedoms, and protections; governmental and societal tolerance for cultural, linguistic, and religious diversity; democratic representation; and unfettered commerce. [emphasis added] (p. 63)

Furthermore, Madrid (1990) asserts that a serious problem now facing the United States, is its high number of illiterate citizens. He argues that, currently, there are over 25 million illiterate people in the United States and the largest majority of these people are English monolingual speakers. Therefore, Madrid (1990) believes that the guardians of the English-only movement should pay attention to the real threat of the nation: illiteracy.

## CONCLUSION

Despite the fact that the United States is one of the few countries in the world which has bilingual programs, the history of bilingual education is very often directed to relations of conquering more advantages for some privileged fractions of society in the context of social and political activities.

Thanks to the struggle of a few groups toward social justice, bilingual education has survived despite the fact that it has also been interpreted as a means of transforming individuals into monologic English speakers under some reactionary policies. Motives and ambitions of language minority groups, for instance, are left behind in history and in actual life. This lack of socio-cultural freedom illustrates the idea that the hegemonic group has no political desire to transform bilingual education into something that leaves the existing position of individual dominant interests. This also represents a strong tendency to restrict democratic rights and to blockade progressive movements within bilingual education. However, it is obvious that social democracy can only arise from social and political conditions without placing some groups in predetermined positions of powerlessness. As David Corson (1993) argues, within his analysis of language policy and social justice, "In promoting social justice in language matters, there is little that can be done for the individual that does not begin with the group at the same time" (p. 28).

# CHAPTER THREE

# WHOSE FINDINGS?

*All the fundamental and essential acts in
human life are brought about by social
stimuli in conditions of a social
environment. If we know only the physical
component of the reaction, we still
understand exceedingly little about a
human act.*
—Voloshinov (1976, p. 22)

Connected to the historical and political aspects of bilingual education are research findings that have impact not only in decisions of reau-
thorizing federal funds but also in analyses regarding what works in
bilingual programs.

The main objective of this chapter is to present a critical analysis of
the existing theoretical approaches and some research findings for bilingual education, from the perspective of the epistemological assumptions of
the Bakhtin circle.

## BILINGUAL EDUCATION AND RESEARCH

### Immersion Programs

The advocates of immersion programs believe this kind of program is beneficial for United Statians and, therefore, it is also beneficial for non-
English speakers in general. For instance, Fred Genesee (1985) writes
about the appropriateness of immersion programs, claiming that they

started in Canada in 1965. Colman Stein (1986) explains that, in 1984, 60 percent of the public school population in Toronto was comprised of non-English-speaking students. Canada is officially bilingual (English and French), but English is the official language in the majority of schools, except in Quebec, where only French instruction is promoted.

Immersion programs in the United States began some time after the first experiences in Canada, more specifically, in California in 1971 (The Culver City Immersion Program). In the United States, immersion programs have different purposes than those in Canada. Genesee (1985) explains that in Canada immersion programs have been applied in schools because of the policies of official bilingualism in the country and because of the bilingual job market. Immersion programs in the United States have been applied for general educational improvement, balanced proportion of ethnolinguistic groups, and accomplishment of some degree of two-way bilingualism in communities where the majority of residents are non-English speakers. However, some scholars (e.g., Clyne, 1972, 1980; Caramazza et al., 1973; Dorian, 1973; Flege and Hillenbrand, 1984) believe that immersion in a second language (L2) can result in the loss of one's native language (L1). This linguistic phenomenon might comprise a loss of proficiency in L1 and can occur when individuals receive a strong influence of L2.

Genesee (1985) notes that The Culver City and The Cincinnati Immersion Programs are successful. He argues that these are programs in which students from diverse socio-economic backgrounds present a high level of functional proficiency in L2 and that none of these students have the same or better performance in L2 as they have in their native language (English).

I would like to discuss some of Genesee's (1985) conclusions about immersion programs. He writes:

> immersion programs were designed for English-speaking students . . . and the evaluation results pertain to this population only. . . . Results indicate that English-speaking students experience no long-term deficits in their English language development as a result of participation in an immersion program. . . . In summary, they [tests] indicate that the immersion approach is a feasible and effective way for English-speaking American students to attain high levels of second language proficiency with-

out risk to their native language development or their academic achievement. (pp. 556–559)

From these conclusions, other conclusions seem relevant. Immersion programs are good for English-speaking students because all of these students are in the same general situation. That is, all of them are learning a language that they do not know. They do not have serious problems later in English because their families are composed of English speakers and because there is no social pressure working against their "speaking consciousness." Therefore, there is little risk for their achievement in English (L1). In fact, these students compose the majority of students in the classroom, but when evaluated they still present problems in L2. This point reinforces some current mistakes in bilingual programs: Non-English- speaking students must be perfect in English as if L2 was their native language. Furthermore, non-English-speaking students have the same evaluations as English-speaking students. This suggests that non-English- speaking students suppress the meanings of both the *words* and the *world* they already know before they go to school. However, a total transformation of a non-English speaker is a great illusion, as Joshua Fishman (1994) argues,

> [l]anguages do not exist independently from the people, families and communities that use them. In other words, language and ethnocultural identity and existence are inextricably linked. . . . When people lose their native language to English, they do not become Anglos and obtain social acceptance. They lose the language as a tool for accessing the help that their families and communities can give them. (p. 28)

After spending several years in a Puerto Rican neighborhood in New York City, Pedro Pedraza and John Attinasi (1980) report in their study of bilingualism that language shift and language maintenance were found in that community. The authors also assert that learning a second language does not mean loss of one's native language but the existence of bilingual skills. On the other hand, there exists an unquestionable aspect of immersion programs: To succeed academically, non-English-speaking students are not living with a temporary change of language, rather they must build quickly a new speaking consciousness.

English-speaking students in immersion programs go back to the meanings of their words and their world in the subject matter at school as soon as they accomplish one or two years of L2. The unfortunate situation for Spanish-speaking students, as well as any other non-English-speaking students, has stemmed from the fact that they are the only ones who must learn a new language without any choice. This means these non-English speakers are the only students who will face difficulties with a new language (L2) among other students who are proficient in English (their L1), who are in the same classroom, and who will not be exposed to a L2 in any of their courses throughout their entire academic life. This is a factor we should consider when we think of immersion programs.

An important characteristic of immersion programs for bilingual education is that the primary language must be simply substituted and new meanings created. In other words, regarding immersion programs, non-English-speaking *students must forget their own speaking consciousness*, at least during the time they are in class. Nevertheless, a word does not exist in itself. Words can exist only within a social significance that includes others and ourselves engaged in the construction of our consciousness. As Bakhtin (1984) remarks,

> [w]hen a member of a speaking collective comes upon a word, it is not a neutral word of language, not as a word free from the aspirations and evaluations of others, uninhabited by others' voices. No, he [or she] receives the word from another's voice and is filled with that other voice. The word enters his [or her] context from another context, permeated with the interpretations of others. (p. 202)

The issue of considering students' contexts within the process of learning is completely relevant. Therefore, let's turn our attention to some theoretical approaches that have been utilized in bilingual education research.

### *Theoretical Approaches to L2 Acquisition*

Kenji Hakuta and Herlinda Cancino (1991) analyze four existing theoretical approaches to L2 acquisition: Contrastive; error; performance; and discourse analysis. These theoretical approaches have been used in bilingual education research.

Hakuta and Cancino (1991) explain that advocates of the *contrastive analysis* (strongly used since the '60s) assume that language development consists in a set of habits. These advocates emphasize that non-English-speaking students' errors stem from the tendency that these students have in transferring habits from the native language to the L2 and that this constitutes a negative interference to the acquisition of a L2. For instance, in Portuguese as well as in Spanish, adjectives come after nouns and the speaker may transfer this understanding to English, saying, for instance, "girl beautiful." This phenomenon represents a cross-linguistic-cultural miscommunication (Connor and Kaplan, 1987; Li and Thompson, 1981).

The second approach addressed by Hakuta and Cancino (1991) is *error analysis*, which stemmed from the impact of Noam Chomsky's theory and from the analysis of intermediate grammars as stages of language acquisition. Error analysis classifies the types of errors presented by non-English speakers during the process of L2 acquisition. According to this analysis, there are two categories of errors: *Interlingual* or interference (the same process as the contrastive analysis) and *intralingual* (aspects of simplification or overgeneralization in grammar use). Hakuta and Cancino (1991) explain that after a test with 179 Spanish-speaking students during the '70s, 5 percent of 513 errors were interlingual and 87 percent were intralingual errors. The authors write the following report:

> [c]ontrastive analysis was, in effect, consumed by error analysis because the evidence of interference errors it used failed to account for the learner's non-interference errors. . . . With increasing sophistication in the methods available to infer knowledge from performance, error analysis is currently in the process of being incorporated within an attempt to describe the learner's overall performance, not necessarily restricting the scope of analysis to errors alone. (pp. 82–83)

To identify the error analysis approach for the purposes of research, non-English-speaking students are placed in specific situations that force them to demonstrate interlingual or intralingual aspects. For instance, Dennis Madrid and Eugene Garcia (1985) analyzed interlingual (or contrastive or transfer) aspects in the speech of sixty Spanish-speaking children through a situation in which the speakers were asked to use negation. For this research, "A complete toy, for example, a car, was shown to the child . . . immediately the child was shown a second car without wheels and asked, 'What's wrong with this car?'" (pp. 58–59). Then, students' sentences were analyzed and classified toward a recognition of those sentences that reflected Spanish construction regarding negation.

The intralingual aspect (overgeneralizations in grammar use), for instance, is a stage that every child has during his or her own native language acquisition and, therefore, can be considered an expected phenomenon for a L2 learner.

Regarding contrastive or interlingual approaches, the process of transferring elements from L1 to L2 is also an example of expected phenomenon, since acquisition of a new language means changes in a speaker's consciousness. In other words, the speaker's linguistic consciousness exists completely impregnated with specific signs (words) that are appropriate to be used in a specific social context—a social context that is responsible for this speaker's awareness. Within the living practice of speech, the linguistic consciousness of speakers-hearers-understanders is not influenced by normative forms of language but with specific contexts in which a determined linguistic form may be applied. As Voloshinov (1973) points out, "A word presents itself not as an item of vocabulary but as a word that has been used in a wide variety of utterances by co-speaker A, co-speaker B, co-speaker C, and so on, and has been variously used in the speaker's own utterances" (p. 70). Therefore, any transference of words and expressions from L1 to L2 means that the speaker's linguistic consciousness, which is social in essence, meets an unknown territory of signs and meanings of L2 and, for this reason, signs of L1 are applied in L2 as if they were appropriate, as if the speaker had not left her or his previous L1 context. In other words, language is inseparable from behavioral and ideological horizons because an utterance is never an end in itself but exists in a level of endless interaction with other utterances as an entire social entity.

From the perspective that an utterance is a social entity, I agree with Gabriele Kasper and Merete Dahl (1991), who present a conclusion that is crucial in terms of interlingual aspects of second language learning. After an analysis of thirty-nine studies of interlanguage pragmatics, Kasper and Dahl (1991) note that the data of interlanguage aspects are difficult to analyze in authentic conversations and that "clearly there is a great need for more authentic data, collected in the full context of the speech event" (p. 245). This means that when language is analyzed outside contextualization, it is, therefore, analyzed outside history (social moment). The main issue here is that a speaker-hearer does not value the form of a word, which is identical in all instances. A speaker-hearer values the context in which the signal (form of a word) becomes a sign according to a specific context. The lack of this perception is what constitutes the antithesis between structural linguistics and the theory that developed out of the Bakhtin circle.

Hakuta and Cancino (1991) continue their analysis to explain the *performance* approach. They report that performance analysis contains refined descriptions of the structures that compose linguistic aspects of children's learning and that research in performance analysis has focused on the acquisition of both negation (when learner's of L2 use sentences such as "Carolina no go to play," which is comparable to a child's first stage of negation: "No Mommy go" or "no eat"); and the use of grammatical morphemes—the appropriate use of articles, auxiliary *be*, and inflections of verbs and nouns—in L2. According to the authors, quantitative research has been helpful to evaluate the degree to which performance is analyzed. Hakuta and Cancino (1991) state that some studies analyzing the performance approach have been conducted, for instance, through a device called a Bilingual Syntax Measure, which consists in a nonspontaneous situation where the subject is asked "to point to each object in a set of cartoon pictures with the request, 'Show me the _____.'" (p. 87). However, the analysis of performance approach is focused on isolated sentences as static elements of language—what constitutes a lack of perceiving the living dialogic word. As Voloshinov emphasizes, it is important to perceive that any utterance is filled with agreements or negations of something because contexts are not homogeneous and exist in a state of constant intercourse and conflictual exchange. Therefore, 'pure' linguistic analysis, as it has been done by structuralist theorists, has no relation to a responsive understanding on the part of the speakers-hearers who are engaged in situations of speech, which are social in essence. This is to say that linguists have a tendency to ignore the mutation of words' evaluative accent according to different contexts in which these words are used. In other words, an utterance cannot be consigned to the level of an isolated item. Descriptions of the structures in performance analysis hide an understanding of the broader conceptual system used by speakers in their social situation (historical moment).

The fourth approach addressed by Hakuta and Cancino (1991) is *discourse analysis*, which investigates the rules of discourse, for instance, in a dialogue. This approach also assumes that language is pragmatic and, therefore, that syntax and semantics are derivations of pragmatic understanding. Hakuta and Cancino (1991) agree that only recently has language and the process of its acquisition been connected to social contexts. The reality of recent educational research on L2 acquisition appears to forget sociolinguistic aspects and the research erroneously concentrates on the quantity of students' errors in L2. This is basically the case of the advocates of contrastive or interlingual analysis. They believe that a contrastive analysis can predict the difficulties in a L2, based on difficulties presented by speakers in their L1. However, what is taken into account is the analysis of disconnected structural factors that are just abstractions of the way in which a language is composed. This perspective of understanding the process of language acquisition is a structural narrow view in which interaction and cross-cultural meanings are left behind. In other words, L2 learners must 'accept' a new language that is not part of their social awareness. Voloshinov brilliantly articulates this idea when he notes that the language teaching of the abstract objectivism is perceived as a ready-made object that is passed from one generation to another. However, nobody receives a ready-made language because everybody penetrates in a long process of constructing both language and consciousness. It is exactly with the beginning of the development of verbal communication that consciousness begins to be developed. Voloshinov (1973) further asserts that "only in learning a foreign language does a fully prepared consciousness— fully prepared thanks to one's native language—confront a fully prepared language which it need only accept. People do not "accept" their native language—it is in their native language that they first reach awareness" (p. 81).

A second language cannot be seen as a ready thing to be swallowed, because language as well as consciousness exists in a process of 'transforming' and 'becoming'. The process of 'accepting' a new language constitutes a process of rebuilding a consciousness—a process in which there exist contrasting contexts. Furthermore, these approaches (contrastive or interlingual; error; intralingual; and discourse analyses) only emphasize grammatical correctness instead of perceiving these contrasts and misuse as expected phenomena within the process of acquiring another language. This grammatical correctness neglects the fact that the utterance is an unstable entity whose focus of concrete meaning depends on social relationships and accents. Therefore, a L2 learner faces new nuances and meanings in the process of accepting a new language.

In bilingual education research, the way in which anxiety plays a powerful role in students' assessment in a second language has been analyzed through statistical measurements (e.g., Scott, 1986; Young, 1991; Phillips, 1992). However, Junil Oh (1992) argues that reading proficiency in second language (L2) has been measured through comprehension questions, thinking out loud, and oral reading, among many other methods, but that the level of students' anxiety about these methods of assessment has been completely ignored. Oh (1992) analyzed what he calls a "homogeneous group in terms of language proficiency" (p. 173), which was composed of eighteen first-year college students who had six years of English (L2) instruction and measured their anxiety in the face of assessment methods. He assumes that familiarity with specific methods determines how much anxiety is provoked. The results of his study illustrate that students present a high level of anxiety when they are not familiar with methods of assessment. Oh also addresses some ways to alleviate students' anxiety, such as discussions with students in classrooms about different methods of assessment. He concludes that students should experience these different methods before their final evaluations.

It seems that these considerations of students' anxiety are too obvious. First of all, we are better prepared for something that we experienced before. Second, despite his recognition of the way in which anxiety plays an important role in students' assessment, Oh (1992) does not consider any assumptions surrounding the multidimensionality of students' lives, such as their social background or the way in which these students perceive themselves within the college arena, the ways in which they learned English, or the ways their cultural background affect their behavioral responses. Students as well as teachers have diverse expectations, shared and unshared views, and find themselves in an unpredictable encounter with diverse motives, self-images, aspirations. Therefore, assessment will never inform the multiple complexities of the learning-teaching process, since classroom interaction is social in essence.

In a quantitative study of children's verbal reasoning performance in a nonnative language, Matthijs Koopmans (1991) reports that, usually, language proficiency is confused with intelligence and that "there has been very little work on the effects of language proficiency on the verbal reasoning of bilingual children" (p. 348). Koopmans's study measured reasoning through syllogisms. (A syllogism is a form of reasoning in which two premises are presented and the individual must present a logical conclusion drawn from them.) Koopmans explains his approach:

All of the cats in the house are Mary's cats.
None of Mary's cats are black.
Are any of the cats in the house black?
To solve this problem, the conclusion needs to be confirmed or

disconfirmed. . . . For the preceding syllogism, a theoretical justification would be:

No, because none of the cats in the house are Mary's.
(justification on the basis of the premises)
An example of an empirical justification is:
No, because Mary is my sister and we don't have a cat at home.
(justification on the basis of empirical knowledge). (p. 349)

For Koopmans's (1991) study, ninety-three Puerto Rican elementary students, who were studying in a bilingual program and who had Spanish as the predominant language spoken at home, were tested in two different sections. In one of these sections, premises were presented in Spanish, in the other section, in English. The students were told they should resolve the problem posited by the premises with answers in Spanish (first section) and in English (second section). Koopmans's study concludes that students' reasoning in Spanish (L1) was better than their reasoning in English (L2). He argues that "in meeting the high processing demands of syllogisms, formal use of the native language appears to be an advantage, whereas solving the syllogisms in English seems to be an additional strain to the child's processing capacities" (p. 354). Koopmans remarks that, "The results of this study indicate that children's level of reasoning ability is not fully reflected in their second-language performance" (p. 356).

Two important questions follow: In what terms can we analyze reasoning? What is reasoning when understood from a linguistic perspective? Koopmans (1991) could easily conjecture that these students would perform better in Spanish because Spanish is the predominant language at home and these students present validity claims that belong to their particular concept of reasoning. The reasoning that they have is the reasoning of their specific context. Their reasoning based on the presented syllogisms had two different levels. In the first section, the students were asked to answer with their native language (L1) while in the second section they were asked to answer in English (L2). This means there are two different processes:

> *First section*: Spanish sentences and meanings—>conclusion with high level of reasoning ability
>
> *Second section*: English sentences—>Spanish meanings—> possible process of distorted translation—> conclusion with not-fully reflected reasoning ability

This means, in turn, that Koopmans's (1991) evaluation of students' reasoning in the second section was based on an ideal speaker's reasoning in a particular context of words and utterances. However, we cannot forget that language is a group of social signs. To reach reasoning, students should perform a process of decoding (an understanding of the relationship among categories that constitute language as a group of codes) to understand the syllogisms presented by Koopmans. Why did some students fail? Perhaps because they had problems in decoding. Perhaps because they did not know how to reach the "appropriate" reasoning without understanding the context of codes. It is worth noting that the process of decoding words is not sufficient to fully guarantee comprehension and, therefore, to reach a desired reasoning. As Voloshinov appropriately remarks, the process of understanding does not signify a recognition of a group of signals which, in the case of Koopmans's second section, are foreign words. The main aspect addressed by Voloshinov is that a process of understanding does not occur if the particular and concrete context in which words and sentences are placed is not considered.

If Koopmans (1991) had questioned the ways in which non-English-speaking students construct reasoning in Spanish (L1) as well as in English (L2), he would not share the simplistic conclusion that reasoning is reached in Spanish but not in English. For this work, Koopmans would first need to understand which meanings and significance students impute to those sentences—that is, how these students understand expressions in Spanish as well as in English. Therefore, the researcher would reach a broader view of the multiple connotations of words and sentences according to the speaker's consciousness. In this sense I agree with Bakhtin's (1981) view that linguists "have taken into consideration only those aspects . . . that take the listener for a person who passively understands but not who actively answers and reacts" (p. 280). Bakhtin reinforces the position that responsive understanding is a primordial essence of the discursive process and that linguists have valued a passive understanding of discourse. Therefore, when we perceive that reading is an act of communication, which is social in nature and in essence, we perceive that this act is not a mere exercise of decoding the words of a text or a passive understanding of a group of codes but a continuous negotiation of meanings that are based on interactive concerns. This view is completely neglected by structuralists who understand that a word or group of words can exist in an isolated framework with a single intention and reception. This narrow, crystallized view limits a broader discussion of the potential dynamic interrelation between *reported speech* and *reporting context*.

As we have seen in chapter 1 of this book, Voloshinov argues that the main aspect of communication is the way in which the reception of a speaker's speech—reported speech— occurs in another speaker's speech— reporting context. This dynamic interrelationship between speaker-hearer and hearer-speaker captures the whole dynamism of social intercourses within any kind of communication. Therefore, this perception establishes a crucial implication for bilingual education research, since any linguistic construction exists within the dialogic nature of language. In other words, Voloshinov offers an insightful theoretical support for researchers to understand that meaning is never alone but exists within living social interrelation. How can we analyze reasoning through responses following from isolated syllogisms? What is missed is that an understanding of a word as well as any utterance is not a one-sided act. As Bakhtin (1981) remarks, in the process of understanding a word what is important is a broader perception of the conditions in which this word occurs and a per- ception of who is speaking. From this perception, one can determine meaning for that speech according to her or his own social position, condi- tion, and also according to the concrete situation. Consequently, a word or an utterance is an elaborated kaleidoscope of meanings and nuances instead of a representation of a static and immutable structure. Within a stable and immutable structure, a word remains a signal. To become a sign and, therefore, passive of understanding, a signal must be oriented in a context.

Studying the process of teaching-learning language, Belle Tyndall (1991) demonstrates that teachers tend to confuse maturity of expression with grammatical correctness even when the learning is another variant of the same language. According to her linguistic analysis of thirty high school Caribbean students' compositions, Tyndall explains that teachers are not aware of the differences between students' English with degrees of Creole and Standard English and that they tend to focus their evaluations on grammatical errors rather than on the content of the compositions. Tyndall (1991) writes: "The fact that teachers are preoccupied with gram- matical mistakes does not mean that they consider content and organiza- tion to be less important. It simply means that they see their primary task as that of helping students to acquire competence in Standard Written English" (p. 200). On the one hand, the judges who were responsible for correcting those thirty compositions understood maturity as absence of grammatical errors. On the other hand, Tyndall endorsed grammatical correctness when she says morphological and syntactic factors are aspects of maturity of expression as well as coherence and cohesive organization. However, I understand that morphological and syntactic constructions are part of grammatical correctness while, contrarily, maturity of expression is related to coherence and the cohesive organization of the thought (Labov, 1972).

A myriad of studies (e.g., Back, 1987; Perini, 1986; Luft, 1985; Halliday, 1974) have shown that language teaching centered on correctness of grammar (syntactic aspects) and spelling (morphological aspects) does not favor an analysis of the presentation of ideas—a perspective that was missed in Tyndall's analysis. This is an example that the traditionalist perspective of language that views communication as external to social context has not changed radically from earlier years. In fact, structural linguistics has been the major source of analyzing one's language development. Here, the theories addressed by Noam Chomsky play a relevant role.

First, Chomsky (1988) believes social reality has little influence on individuals' language acquisition.

> Acquisition of language is something that happens to you; it's not something that you do. Learning language is something like undergoing puberty. You don't learn to do it; you don't do it because you see other people doing it; you are just designed to do it at a certain time. . . . There are social factors that determine rate and timing and so forth, but overwhelmingly what is happening is that the biological process is proceeding in the way in which it is determined to proceed. When we study natural human functions, like the development of conceptual systems, and basic ways of thinking and interpreting the physical and social world around us, then it's very much like studying puberty. (p. 174)

Furthermore, Chomsky asserts that knowledge of a language can be explicit in the system of rules (grammar) that produces language. When individuals have this system in mind, they can create an infinite set of sentences. Chomsky (1965) also argues that speakers acquire and internalize a generative grammar (system of rules that connects signals to interpretations of these signals) that indicates the knowledge of their language.

Furthermore, he assumes speakers have an intuitive knowledge of their language.

Chomsky (1977) explains that knowledge of a language is characterized by the knowledge of the grammar of a particular language: "The grammar assigns to each possible linguistic expression (this, a notion of Universal Grammar) a structural description, which consists of a representation of this expression on each level of linguistic description" (p. 3). In other words, an individual who knows language has a system of pragmatic competence that allows this individual to know how to use language. Therefore, Chomsky addresses a distinction between *competence* and *performance* or, in other words, between what an individual knows implicitly (competence) and what she or he uses in communicative interaction (performance). It is in the competence that there exists what Chomsky (1977) calls "creativity of language, that is, the speaker's ability to produce new sentences, that are immediately understood by other speakers" (p. 8). For Chomsky, the rules of grammar contain a myriad of separate cognitive structures with their specific characteristics, which exist in constant interaction with the production and interpretation of speech and reactions of individuals. Therefore, regarding the use of language (performance), Chomsky (1971) argues that the normal use of language embraces interpretation and the production of sentences that stem from a set of rules of the same grammar.

What is missing in Chomsky's analysis is that language exists for the purposes of communication which happens in social contexts. For this reason, I disagree with Chomsky when he argues that learning a language is a biological process like puberty. I also believe the problem with Chomsky's theory is not the idea that individuals must utilize a specific set of rules in the process of communication but that the knowledge of a language is analyzed through the competence and performance of an *ideal speaker-hearer.* This assumption presumes that the knowledge of a language means being adequate to the parameters of this idealized speaker-hearer who exists only in abstraction and who has been considered as an appropriate standard for evaluations. This is also the key concept that has been used for empirical evaluation of one's knowledge of language, especially a second language. If we think of the ways in which L2 acquisition is considered by schools, we will realize that the general imperative of bilingual education has been a mere memorization of names, expressions, and so forth. In this sense, I completely agree with Voloshinov when he notes that signalization is important in language but, when acquiring a second language, the recognition of signalization is not sufficient to assert that this "second language" became language. As Voloshinov (1973) argues, *"What is central to all these methods* [methods of teaching foreign languages] *is that students become acquainted with each linguistic form only in concrete contexts and situations"* (p. 69).

Students begin an engagement in the process of responsive understanding only when they can experience a word in diverse contexts because they need chances of perceiving the contextual diversity and changeability of signs. It is obvious that the form (signal) of a specific word is relevant but form is nothing if compared to the ways in which this specific form can be a mutable sign. For this reason, I believe that when language is studied through a structural analysis of disconnected sentences, the social dynamism between speaker and hearer is lost and, therefore, the encounter of individuals' social consciousness is also lost. To relate the speaker's and hearer's (another speaker) perspectives to the content of consciousness means an understanding of this speaker's and hearer's social background. Therefore, it is impossible to consider an ideal speaker-hearer because such an individual does not exist at all.

Rogelio Diaz-Guerrero and Lorand Szalay (1991) illustrate the importance of considering social background as a crucial factor in second language acquisition. They explain cultural factors (through an extensive empirical data) that elucidate significant differences (I would say "nuances" ignored in schools) in the way that groups perceive and evaluate the same words and expressions. For instance, the word *power* in English is *poder* in Spanish. Basically, the word has the same meaning for United Statians and Mexicans, but the difference goes beyond linguistic semantic aspects. Among other differences, power for United Statians strongly means political and international relations. United Statians think about world power while Mexicans present a more domestic perspective of power and relate this word to abuse of power, such as exploitation and social injustices. The authors write that power "was found to be better, more powerful, active and meaningful for Americans than Mexicans" (p. 183).

Another example concerns the meaning of *teacher* in English and *maestro* in Spanish. According to Diaz-Guerrero and Szalay (1991), United Statians and Mexicans both perceive a teacher as someone who is part of the school, but the difference is United Statians present "a narrower focus on the teacher's characteristics and technical functions, while Mexican students see the teacher from a less technical, more human

angle" (p. 133). This means that, in schools, Mexican students interpret
English words in a way that is different from the monolingual English
speaker. As Voloshinov (1973) argues, "One is sensible of one's native
word in a completely different way or, to be more precise, one is ordinarily
not sensible of one's native word" (p. 75). Regarding the analysis of a word
or sentence, the lack of sensibility between two individuals who speak different languages exists because what is at stake is not a mere recognition of
diverse signals but signals within specific 'contextualization'; in other
words, signals within orientation in the dynamism of language usage—the
living existence of signs.

The lack of understanding that the word usage in diverse contexts
does not occur in equal planes and that utterances in these contexts are not
previously circumscribed pointing to an equal direction is, according to
Voloshinov, one of the major problems of the abstract objectivism.
Therefore, any attempt toward mere memorization of vocabulary and
grammatical constructions or linguistic differences can guarantee neither
learning nor understanding if cultural aspects of a student's native language are not taken into account.

Differences in cultural meanings also exist within the relationship
among students, parents, and schools. Beth Harry (1992), as a result of her
study of Puerto Rican families, argues that parents of non-English-
speaking students do not question school authority because they believe
that they are not expected to participate in decision making and that they
must demonstrate respect and trust for school authorities. This sense of
respect is translated into a passive attitude of acceptance. Harry (1992)
utilized interviews and observations to analyze parent-professional interaction in a cross-cultural context. The participants of her study were
twelve Spanish-speaking Puerto Rican families whose children were classified as disabled. Harry (1992) writes that

> [t]his deference was often misunderstood by professionals, as
> typified by the following comment by a school social worker:
> "They [parents] come to the meetings and agree to everything,
> and then they go away and say they do not like the decisions that
> were made." Many parents, however, explained that they found
> it difficult to disagree openly with professionals because of their
> perceived status. For example, Ana could not bring herself to
> express to school personnel her strong objection to what she
> perceived as a repetitive and unchallenging curriculum in Gina's

self-contained class. "After all," she said, "that is the teacher!" The identical phrase was used by several mothers in the study. This pattern is reminiscent of what Bennett has called 'the face of respeto' ('respect') shown to professionals by even the most critical parents. (p. 480)

For these parents, the U.S. school system seems uncaring and impersonal because teachers do not care for the children and their personal problems but only for what the children have to learn. This way of seeing the educational system affects the way in which non-English-speaking students work in schools. However, we cannot forget that individuals react ideologically and behaviorally within any context in which words are used. In the case of Harry's research, while *agreement* (a word-reaction) means 'respect' for a group, it also means 'lack of interest' or 'negative reaction' for another group. In this view, it is important to observe that within the same specific social context (school meetings) both groups—with divergent social backgrounds/contexts—bring out a divergent significance and ideological criterion to establish meaning. From this point of view, Voloshinov (1973) states, "Any act of understanding is a response, i.e., it translates what is being understood into a new context from which a response can be made" (p. 69).

A successful fulfillment of the teaching-learning process requires an understanding of the students' cultural repertoire. This is the issue that has been left behind in terms of bilingual programs and research. For instance, in an ethnographic research, Martha Crago (1992) studied the role of cultural context in the communicative interaction of Inuit students in Canada. Crago explains that during kindergarten and grades one and two, these students are taught in Inuktitut (their L1). After the second grade, they receive instruction in either French or English. The choice of a second language is made by the students' parents. Crago (1992) argues that non-Inuit teachers indicated that more than 30 percent of their students have language disabilities because they do not talk in class. However, what is missed is that, in Inuit culture, children are considered well-raised when they learn by looking and listening. That is, they are not supposed to talk in class.

Research in bilingual education indicates the positive effects of student talk and interaction on second language acquisition (e.g., Long and Porter, 1985; Doughty and Pica, 1986). For instance, John Green (1993) analyzes the ways in which students perceive English as a Second

Language (ESL) programs. The subjects of his study were 263 Puerto Rican students who were attending the second semester of intermediate ESL. According to Green (1993), students experienced "a variety of teaching methods and activities, but that noncommunicative methods had been experienced somewhat more frequently than communicative ones" (p. 4) despite students' consideration that oral communicative methods are more enjoyable. However, these overgeneralizations in research findings cannot be applied to Inuit children, for instance, who are not expected to participate or ask questions when adults are talking. Crago (1992) clarifies that in their community, these children are told they can neither participate nor ask questions because they are small and young. For instance, Inuit men learn to hunt through observation and cannot ask questions until they can hunt by themselves. Crago (1992) notes that learning in the Inuit culture occurs by overhearing the conversations and stories of adults—questions are not even tolerated. Therefore, cultures have diverse intentions and diverse meanings of communication. Among many peculiarities, Crago (1992) states that Inuit adults do not ask children to name objects when they begin to say their first words—children are expected just to be spectators.

It is obvious that the patterns of communication used by Inuits enter into an arena of conflict when these children face the kind of communicative interaction requested by teachers in public school and approved by standard research findings. Cultural identity is rarely considered by teachers of second language and, therefore, Inuit children are evaluated as linguistically disabled. I completely agree with Crago (1992) who argues, "The teaching and learning of a second language may lead to more successful outcomes for the children involved if research and educational efforts continue to explore the cultural and communicative dimensions of second language learning" (p. 502). This means a comprehension of nondominant cultures and the way in which people understand the world is necessary for any kind of bilingual programs.

In fact, the teaching-learning process in bilingual education has been focused on whether or not grammar instruction is appropriate for non-English-speaking students (e.g., Vanpatten and Cadierno, 1993; Glisan and Drescher, 1993), based on an ideal English speaker's performance. Furthermore, much of the standard research in bilingual education has shown basically one way to perceive research: Usually, there is a group of students who are tested and evaluated according to their performance in English—performance that is understood as "appropriate" scores in writing and reading. This narrow sense of research is limited and opposed to the Bakhtin circle's assumptions about language as a social entity.

Language as a social entity embraces the idea that the ideological environment is reflected in the way in which one acquires a second language. In other words, individuals are inseparable parts of ideologies that compose their social-historical situation. Therefore, there is no such thing as the moment of writing or the moment of reading without considering contextual influences that engage the speaker in conflicting and multifaceted ways of understanding, as Bakhtin (1981) argues:

> What we have in mind here is not an abstract linguistic minimum of a common language, in the sense of a system of elementary forms (linguistic symbols) guaranteeing a minimum level of comprehension in practical communication. We are taking language not as a system of abstract grammatical categories, but rather language conceived as ideologically saturated, language as a world view, even as a concrete opinion, insuring a maximum of mutual understanding in all spheres of ideological life. (p. 271)

Furthermore, standard studies present an arbitrary system of evaluations that have no relation to the cultural-social background of students. The central issue becomes acceptability of parameters toward a judgment of what is right and what is wrong. For instance, Graham Crookes (1991) argues that in language acquisition research "the second language speech production model is assumed (usually implicitly) to be basically the same as that for L1 production" (p. 116). This implicit assumption constitutes an enormous mistake because the process of acquiring a native language is a process of building social consciousness and awareness. On the other hand, *the process of acquiring a second language means that a previously constructed consciousness will face a completely different context of signs; that is, new social-ideological meanings.* Regarding speech, Voloshinov (1973) calls our attention to the fact that "forms of speech interchange operate in extremely close connection with the conditions of the social situation in which they occur" (p. 20). Therefore, how can we consider the speech production model of L1 as equal to L2?

Another serious problem in standard research is that some researchers believe a group of students can be considered homogeneous just because they belong to the same classroom or academic level (e.g., Kobayashi, 1992; Roller and Matambo, 1992; Cervantes and Gainer, 1992; Carrell, 1987; Nunan, 1987). In addition, from these homogeneous assumptions, standard research in bilingual education has demonstrated an obsession to understand what factors affect the low performance of non-English-speaking students, such as diverse levels of cognitive aspects (e.g., Landry, 1974; Segalowitz, 1977; Humphrey, 1977; Abraham, 1983; Chapelle and Roberts, 1986; Chamot and O'Malley, 1987); age (e.g., Krashen et al., 1979; Izzo, 1981; Collier, 1987; Abella, 1992); and reading problems (e.g., Rosenthal et al., 1983; So and Chan, 1984), instead of an understanding of the cultural dimensions that permeate students' lives or what these students are able to do. In other words, *students' language ability is usually measured through scores of second language tests or through fictional situations of speech.* In fact, a comparison of the amount of knowledge of non-English speakers with what is expected from an English-standard speaker is emphasized throughout these studies. This perspective neglects the fact that communities are not homogeneous and that students receive influences other than standard English.

Beyond the limited analysis of communicative levels in second language, there exists in the standard research of bilingual education a tendency to overlook the effects of cultural disruptions experienced by non-English-speaking students and their families. For instance, Fernando Gutiérrez (1985) argues that manifestations of cultural shock "can be experienced in the form of shyness, withdrawal, and irritability" (p. 108) and that, frequently, non-English-speaking families find a balance between alienation and conformity. After an analysis of case studies of non-English-speaking students and their families, Gutiérrez (1985) explains that

> [a]s immigrants or ethnic group members conform to the host culture, they may realize that the reason for conforming is a sense of shame for being culturally different. . . . At the same time, they are also feeling shame for having conforming, since this is viewed by the ethnic group and family members, usually the parents, as betrayal. . . . Being able to function in both cultures is not something innate, but is learned through a long and sometimes painstaking process. (pp. 110–122)

These cultural disruptions have an undeniable strong influence on one's second language acquisition within a myriad of stages of acculturation. For this reason, I believe that questions dealing with the ways in which non-English-speaking students think they construct their knowledge, what these students think about the bilingual program in which they are enrolled, how they interpret their experiences in classrooms; and how they shape their own development in second language, as a way of resistance, are left behind in standard research and daily practices of bilingual education.

It is argued that the validity and reliability of an instrument used in standard research can be indicated by statistical procedures. Once this instrument presents considerable levels of validity and reliability, it is ready to analyze students' proficiency in a language. However, the fact that in standard research the parameters of knowledge are conventionalized according to one's assumptions of what is considered relevant cannot be rejected. An example of the inappropriateness of these parameters in standard research is addressed by Ann Willig (1985) in her meta-analysis of selected studies on the effectiveness of bilingual education.

Meta-analysis consists in a statistical analysis of numerous research findings. Ann Willig (1985) analyzed twenty-three randomly selected studies that were focused on the effects of bilingual education on the learning of a second language. Willig (1985) argues that these studies presented "inequitable comparisons between bilingual program students and students that differed in language dominance and/or their need for a bilingual program" (p. 277). Furthermore, she asserts that language tests have low levels of reliability and validity, and that these studies reflect uncontrolled differences between experimental and comparison groups of students. In this sense, a quantitative analysis of students' proficiency in a second language has not only internal arbitrary inconsistency but hinders the influence of cultural assumptions when these students are evaluated in the so-called very moment when they are writing or speaking, without considering what comprises their social moment, their historical situation. Furthermore, David Nunan (1991) analyzed fifty empirical investigations of teaching and learning in second language. Nunan (1991) notes that

> it is evident from this review that little second language research is actually carried out in language classrooms, and that we know comparatively little about what does or does not go on there. The existence, and indeed persistence, of this state of ignorance may seem surprising given the frequency with which attempts are made to import into second language classrooms insights from research conducted outside the classroom. (p. 265)

Nunan's analysis is completely relevant because he is making reference to the process of teaching-learning second language. In other words, there is no reason to get insights from outside the classroom if these insights are not used throughout the process of teaching-learning. There is no reason to do research if analyses are not used toward transformations of methodologies. At the same time, it is necessary to have a larger vision of "what is going on" in second language classes. However, the dimension of the development in any process of learning cannot be just measured on the basis of tests—this is what is overlooked in standard research. Following this perspective, I share Voloshinov's (1973) view when he remarks that

[w]ith each attempt to delimit the object of investigation, to reduce it to a compact subject-matter complex of definitive and inspectable [*sic*] dimensions, we forfeit the very essence of the thing we are studying—its semiotic and ideological nature. . . . In order to observe the process of combustion, a substance must be placed into the air. In order to observe the phenomenon of language, both the producer and the receiver of sound and the sound itself must be placed into the social atmosphere. (p. 46)

The main difference between quantitative and qualitative approaches for research is addressed by Yvonna Lincoln and Egon Guba (1985) when they argue that, for the qualitative research "there are multiply constructed realities" (p. 37) and for quantitative researchers "there is a single tangible reality 'out there'" (p. 37). Therefore, there is no generalization in the qualitative approach, and a small number of students are not considered as representative of the whole population of students. For this reason, I believe the quantitative approach offers a limited and, sometimes, distorted analysis of students' proficiency in language because it is, basically, focused on overgeneralizations. However, the results that have been utilized to evaluate the appropriateness of bilingual programs (including its maintenance) are presented through these standard methods.

A qualitative approach offers the possibility of uncovering sociocultural factors that are crucial to one's consciousness. On the other hand, Richard Quantz and Terence O'Connor (1988) say that

[t]here has been a strong tendency among ethnographers to describe complex, historical, social activities as homogeneous, rule-governed, ahistorical entities. This ethnographic tradition has reinforced a conception of culture as a single, unified set of patterns passed down from generation to generation which governs life within a community. Such a conception masks the dynamic and conflictual nature of culture in pluralistic societies and effectively reinforces the idea that education must be reproductive rather than transformative. (p. 95)

Advocates of standard as well as interpretive paradigms need to reach an understanding of the way in which both paradigms can address the complexities of second language acquisition without the illusion that people have had the same experiences just because they belong to a certain group.

## CONCLUSION

The study of people at one specific place and time can give us a very limited view of the whole social dimension in which individuals exist. Furthermore, this limited view cannot be applied to all groups even if these groups belong to the same society. Therefore, any thoughtful educational research should consider the contradictions that exist in the process of acquiring any kind of knowledge. Any collection of abstract beliefs supported by facts in isolation can represent an exclusion of living and historical social experience. Following this perspective, one important contribution of the Bakhtin circle to bilingual education research is a broader comprehension of the ways in which meaning is created. In other words, by viewing the construction of *meaning* as the effect of interaction among people, researchers acquire an essential vantage point from which to analyze intercultural characterization through a research approach that can give more than 'wrongs' and 'rights' as its results.

A bilingual education researcher must consider a perspective on research that embraces an acknowledgment of the mechanisms from which second language learners confront diverse contexts. For this reason, Voloshinov's analysis of *reported speech* and *reporting context* is fundamental for bilingual education research. This analysis is fundamental to delineate the dimensions in which a community modifies the social reception of any reported speech and also to analyze the ways in which the expressiveness of speech is comprehended as socially relevant or even divergent to that community.

When we think of language through a social-semiotic perspective, we do not see language as a formal system but as a medium for social life (Halliday and Hasan, 1985). Within this perspective, Voloshinov (1973) presents an interesting metaphor to illustrate this point when he writes that those "who, in attempting to define the meaning of a word, approach its lower, stable, self-identical limit, want, in effect, to turn on a light bulb after having switched off the current" (p. 103). Therefore, if the functional existence of language is the embodiment of social-ideological meanings, language comprises more than disconnected sentences to be analyzed by linguists. This constitutes another major contribution of the Bakhtin circle regarding research findings in bilingual education. By viewing research as a means of understanding that language is not static and that *speakers-hearers exist within social-cultural effervescence*, researchers have a necessary theoretical support to become involved in the development, changes, interdependence, and experiences of second language learners.

An individual is social and, therefore, cannot be considered as a unique and independent entity. Rather, an individual is a social response that follows from her or his social consciousness. Consequently, students cannot be considered as a body of homogeneous consciousness (a dominant perspective of standard research) as if diverse social accents, such as the diverse effects of one's ethnicity and cultural background, do not exist in society. As Joshua Fishman (1994) properly argues, "Language-minority groups want more than tolerance, token programs, and 'transitional aspirin'. They want cultural democracy" (p. 29).

# CHAPTER FOUR

# LANGUAGE AND ITS MULTIPLE VOICES

*We are more inclined to imagine ideological
creation as some inner process of understanding, comprehension, and perception,
and do not notice that it in fact unfolds
externally, for the eye, the ear, the hand.
It is not within us, but between us.*
—Medvedev (1978, p. 8)

As we have seen in this book, the major critique addressed by the
Bakhtin circle regarding structural linguistics is that linguists present a
restricted semiotic understanding of language. Linguists tend to perceive
the sign as a ready-made "code" and as a part of an abstract system. As Ken
Hirschkop (1989b) argues, "The society we find in Saussure is a disturbingly homogeneous collective . . . in which every subject behaves
according to formal rules, to be obeyed without reference to ends, values or
mitigating circumstances" (p. 8). On the other hand, for the Bakhtin circle, language must be considered as a semiotic social-cultural entity which
stems from the dynamic process of history. In this sense, language
becomes a semiotic social-cultural entity that is dialogically alive and
mutable.

According to the Bakhtin circle, an analysis of language is, first of all,
an analysis of its ideological-semiotic value and the way in which language, as a changeable sign, is a site for the embodiment of ideologies.
From this perspective, the process of communication among people,
which is the reason for language's existence, must be perceived as a social

accomplishment of the ideological sign. The semiotic standpoint does not exist outside of social interaction in which consciousness meets consciousness. In other words, each word we use, in whatever language, is a group of signals that does not have sense in itself, only because it is a social convention (when signals become signs)—a social semiotic embodiment of ideologies. Therefore, Bakhtinian[1] theory emphasizes that language is not passively assimilated by an individual; rather, language is a dynamic process that exists dynamically in the socio-historical arena. The main idea I wish to emphasize is not an understanding of isolated words but an understanding of the utterance which has its foundation and existence in social relations. As David Danow (1991) points out, "In this view, not only does the subject lend specificity to his [or her] utterance, but so does another's reaction, another's word" (p. 22). In this sense, language is never a consummated outcome but a dynamic social entity and, therefore, a socio-cultural phenomenon.

When disconnecting langue from parole, the Saussurean perspective, which is still the most dominant in linguistic study, concentrates on morphology, phonology, syntax, and semantics as distinctive parts of language without placing emphasis on language within socio-ideological contexts. As Saussure (1959) remarks, "The true and unique object of linguistics is language studied in and for itself" (p. 232). However, as we have seen in chapter 1 of this book, the Bakhtin circle argues against Saussurean notions of language because these notions do not give consideration to the fact that both language and social contexts shape people's identity. For this reason, the Bakhtin circle emphasizes social and cultural interrelations as crucial factors to analyze language.

The study of language as our cultural and social existence is something that has been neglected, especially in bilingual education. The structuralist assumptions about language are reflected in established ideas about teaching-learning within bilingual education. In other words, there exists a tendency to believe that students have to learn a language as if they do not use language before they go to school. Their speaking consciousness and their cultural background are often rejected as a possible contribution to the process of learning. In fact, the structuralist view of language neglects a *dialogic-linguistics*, which gives serious consideration to the historical location of the utterance.

---

1. Bakhtinian will be used to refer to the theory addressed by the Bakhtin circle.

I am not using the term *dialogic-linguistics* to refer to existing sociolinguistics. Usually, sociolinguistics has been dedicated to the study of diverse dialects within a specific culture and "the ways in which the speakers draw upon the resources of their language to perform certain functions" (Labov, 1991, p. 184). Dialogic-linguistics, in the Bakhtinian sense, considers not only the actual moment of the community but its historical location/context. For instance, if a researcher is analyzing a specific culture, she cannot neglect the factor of cultural interrelation; that is, how aspects such as the multifaceted/multiaccentuated language of this culture addresses ideological changes within the movement of historical transformation. Following this idea, I agree with Susan Stewart (1986) who argues that

> [w]hereas such studies as William Labov's on the social implications of sound-change vindicate Bakhtin's rejection of a purely "linguistic" conception of phonology, the majority of sociolinguistic studies tends, no less problematically, to emphasize context in a highly abstract way—that is, without a corresponding discussion of the location of the utterance in history and social life. . . . And although Bakhtin presents an investigation of utterances in context, his concern with dialogue, with conflict, and, especially, with the cumulative forces of history acting upon each speech situation distinguishes his work from contemporary sociolinguistic theories. (pp. 45–46)

Existing trends in mainstream sociolinguistic studies dismiss the assumption that "beliefs and values are not static but dynamic, determined by the historically evolving mode of existence characteristic of given communities" (Gardiner, 1992, p. 15). Therefore, a dialogic-linguistics would neither define a specific culture within its boundaries of speech nor place an emphasis on rule-governed behavior because it recognizes the multifaceted existence of language. Dialogic-linguistics, in the Bakhtinian sense, makes room for the development of "a concept of culture that recognizes the complex contradictions within societies and, therefore, makes the idea of transformative education possible" (Quantz and O'Connor, 1988, p. 95). It is relevant to remember that the process of understanding, which implies judgment, does not occur within cultural consensus since the struggle among diverse accentualities (social interests) has the potential to challenge dominant meanings.

Regarding the analysis of language, the main aspect addressed by the Bakhtin circle concerns the relevance of the dialogical characteristic of language. Language, as any other ideological sign, exists only if it can be understood through the perspective of the social and cultural—both aspects that are forged in history. In fact, language flows within social exchange—an exchange of consciousness that establishes the dialogical relationship between the speaker and the listener (who is another speaker). In this sense, the theory developed by the Bakhtin circle represents a deconstruction (in a postmodern sense) of the idea that an individual is the owner of her or his own utterances, since the concrete owner of language is, in fact, the social arena. As Bakhtin (1981) argues, "There are no 'neutral' words and forms—words and forms that can belong to 'no one'. . . . As a living, socio-ideological concrete thing . . . language, for the individual consciousness, lies on the borderline between oneself and the other" (p. 293). Therefore, language can never be analyzed outside social, historical, and cultural human existence.

## DIALOGUE: WHAT IS IT?

According to Bakhtinian theory, *an individual does not exist outside of dialogue*—a dialogue in which the consciousness of a speaker encounters the consciousness of another speaker; a dialogue that reveals conflicts; a dialogue that embodies history and culture; and therefore, a dialogue that is multifaceted. This view of dialogue considers the social location that constructs the self and the other. Through an understanding of dialogical human existence, it is possible to perceive why language is an embodiment of ideologies and why it is important to consider the social and cultural contexts.

To understand the meaning of dialogue in the Bakhtinian sense, it is important that we challenge our perception of dialogue as it has usually been used. Here, dialogue is not only a conversation between two people. In the Bakhtinian sense, dialogue goes beyond oral communication—dialogue is what guarantees our existence.

In the Bakhtinian sense of dialogue, two aspects are mutually inclusive: *the self* and *the other*. The existence of the self and the other is a simultaneous existence; a dialogical existence. The Bakhtinian notion of language embraces the idea that the other cannot be silenced or excluded. Within this assumption, nonstandard speakers, for instance, are not only part of heteroglossic/multiaccentuated language but also contribute to maintaining the dialogical existence of language. This notion rejects monologic forms and opposes monoglossia to heteroglossia. Monoglossic standard language and the way in which it is diffused in schools, for instance, places individuals in hierarchical positions. In other words, the languages that many students bring to the classroom are omitted within the teaching-learning process since the standard/monologic language assumes an evaluation of which languages are appropriate and which languages must be marginalized.

Because of the existence of heteroglossia, *language must be understood as a site of political struggle in which meanings collide and have to be negotiated*. This struggle is composed of diverse accents and multiple locations. However, Tony Crowley (1989) argues that an emphasis on heteroglossia reinforces mechanisms of domination. His argument is based on a comparison between Bakhtin's and Antonio Gramsci's theories. Crowley writes that

> [Gramsci's] work takes a theoretical and practical line distinct from that of Bakhtin; Gramsci's argument is that in the historical and political conjuncture in which he was located, rather than arguing for heteroglossia, what was required was precisely the organising force of a monoglossia. . . . In a situation in which a linguistic hierarchy exists, a refusal to work for common and unified forms is a tantamount to support for an unjust distribution of power. . . . The preference for pluralism and difference may well be a laudable one: but history demonstrates that forms of unity and organisation may be a prerequisite before such an achievement can be attained. (pp. 84–85)

Furthermore, Crowley (1989) asserts that the reasons for Bakhtin's emphasis on heteroglossia and Gramsci's emphasis on monoglossia stem from the fact that these theorists faced different realities. While Bakhtin experienced cruel forms of unification, Gramsci experienced a multifactional, popular mass that was lost within its plurality.

Despite the fact that the political situations experienced by Bakhtin and Gramsci were very different from each other, Crowley's (1989) analysis reinforces the Bakhtinian notion that language never exists outside historical forces and that the dialogic essence of language implies that a unique group can never dominate all other languages completely. This refers to both counter-hegemony and heterogeneity. Both Gramsci and

Bakhtin argue that diverse languages cannot be suppressed and that there exists a standard/monologic language that struggles to maintain its position of domination. As Gramsci (1988) clarifies,

> the entire 'educated class', with its intellectual activity, is detached from people-nation. . . . A national popular literature, narrative or other kinds, has always been lacking in Italy and still is. . . . The lay forces have failed in their historical task. . . . They have been incapable of satisfying the intellectual needs of the people precisely because they have failed to represent a lay culture . . . they have been tied to an antiquated world, narrow, abstract, too individualistic or caste-like. (pp. 368–369)

Therefore, the heterogeneity of language or its heteroglossic existence becomes a way toward effecting a 'de-hierarchization' of language. As Pierrette Malcuzynski (1990) points out, this involves "a practice of dehierarchization where the producing subject is itself understood as the product of dialogized instances with other socio-cultural subjects" (p. 89). Following this perspective, both Bakhtin and Gramsci value the multifaceted aspect of culture and language within the social-political existence. Each recognizes that even in a single culture language constitutes the multiplicity that exists between the social and the individual. Viewed as such, a monologic/standard language is a mere abstraction. As Bakhtin analyzes, language cannot be seen as unitary because the only way of seeing language as unitary and in complete isolation from the larger social process of becoming is through an abstract linguistics. The unique and immutable system of grammatical norms exists only outside the living language/existence. On the other hand, a myriad of worlds challenge this abstract immutable sense of language because no one can reduce the boundaries of socio-ideological belief systems.

Although two people live in the same community, meanings are always relative because meanings always depend on the relationship among these people and their location in the community. Dialogical existence means existence is both perceived and experienced by an individual. Within this existence, an individual is an active participant as well as a spectator—a spectator who perceives and who is, at the same time, perceived. This is what is meant by the dialogical existence of the self and the other. Furthermore, this perception takes place in time and space, which comprise the arena of simultaneity. Michael Holquist (1990) addresses one of Bakhtin's examples to illustrate this point.

> He begins with a simple datum from experience; not an observer looking at trains, but an observer looking at another observer. You can see things behind my back that I cannot see, and I see things behind your back that are denied to your vision. We are both doing essentially the same thing, but from different places: although we are in the same event, that event is different for each of us. (p. 21)

Consequently, I do not perceive myself as the other perceives me and vice-versa, despite both selves occupying the same place at the same time. However, time and space become oppositional since I can perceive what exists behind the other's back, while I cannot perceive what is behind my back. In other words, I have a limited perception of myself just as the other has a limited perception of herself or himself. In this sense, existence is something shared; it constitutes a coexistence in which the "I" cannot exist without the "other." In other words, we need the perception of others in order to exist. This constitutes the dialogical nature of existence: The "I" exists through the words of "others." For this reason, a Bakhtinian understanding of existence is forged in the existence of the utterance. Furthermore, existence as well as an utterance must be understood as mutable and conflictual. As Holquist (1990) points out, "Bakhtin's metaphor for the unity of the two elements constituting the relation of the self and the other is dialogue, the simultaneous unity of differences in the event of utterance" (p. 36).

It is from the perception of the other that we see ourselves as part of the world. It is from the perception of the other that we cannot reject our own existence. The self does not have sense or meaning in itself, only in relation to the whole of social existence and in relation to other selves. For instance, when we are born we have no idea if we are a woman or a man. The construction of ourselves is based on the other's perception. Without the social and cultural, the self ceases to exist. Following this idea, dialogue must be understood as multiple perceptions and locations, which could be called a "multilogue" comprising our existence. Existence as well as language is not an isolated phenomenon but a dynamic social phenomenon.

Within this dynamic social phenomenon, the sign is something mutable and unstable. For instance, in chapter 1 of this book, I mentioned the difference between signal and sign through an analysis of the Brazilian flag, in which the color green represents the forests and the color white represents peace. However, these signs offer a myriad of meanings depending on one's historical and social location. To me, the color green represents the forests that have been destroyed and the color white represents a peace that the Brazilian population did not experience during more than twenty years of military dictatorship. Therefore, a sign and its ideological meaning is not static and stable. As "I" exist in a particular time and space, my responses to the signs of the Brazilian flag may differ from the responses of the "other." Therefore, within social contexts, the understanding of ideological signs exists "in a state of constant tension, or incessant interaction and conflict" (Voloshinov, 1973, p. 80). In social existence, signs always request a response and even if we neglect their existence we are still addressing a response. In other words, we are constantly responding and bringing meaning (*the effect of interaction*) to a circumstance that is a dialogical understanding of the sign that does not exist isolated from other signs.

Bakhtinian theory rejects the vision that utterances are monologic because the relationships between the self and the other, and between the individual and the social, are not oppositional relations but dialogical in nature and in essence. From the Bakhtinian perspective, we can understand the existence of plural social relations and the ways in which this social plurality shares a sign.

Since a sign is never a sign unless it is shared, the borderline between the individual and the social does not lie within the dialectical opposition but within the dialogical existence in which the "I" and the "other" coexist. For this reason, we cannot endorse a monologic utterance since language, as comprised of mutable signs, is shared and exists not only for the purposes of communication but also within the construction of 'our-selves'. As we have seen in chapter 1 of this book, Voloshinov constantly argues that language—*utterance*—lives in concrete communication and not in an abstract linguistic system.

> The concrete utterance (and not the linguistic abstraction) is born, lives, and dies in the process of social interaction between the participants of the utterance. Its form and meaning are determined basically by the form and character of this interaction. When we cut the utterance off from the real grounds that nurture it, we lose the key to its form as well as to its import—all

we have left is an abstract linguistic shell or an equally abstract semantic scheme . . . two abstractions that are not mutually joinable because there are no concrete grounds for their organic synthesis. (Voloshinov, 1976, p. 105)

Therefore, a Bakhtinian theory of language is one in which communication is analyzed. It is in the process of communication that meaning and social relations exist in a complete interconnection in which people experience the dialogical existence. Communication is an encounter of utterances; an encounter in which the "I" is the "other" and the "other" is the "I", simultaneously.

It is worth noting that Bakhtinian utterance is not only what is said but also what is not said—*extraverbal context* and *inward speech*. As Voloshinov (1973) points out, "The process of speech, broadly understood as the process of inner and outer verbal life, goes on continuously. It knows neither beginning nor end" (p. 96). Both the historical context and the nonverbal factors are crucial participants of human interaction and dialogic existence. This means even the inner word "has a material and social dimension" (McClellan, 1990, p. 241). Therefore, *otherness* is a key concept to the Bakhtinian notion of language and discourse. In this sense, Pierrette Malcuzynski (1990) explains that "the Bakhtinian subject always considers the 'other' an interlocutor, a fully embodied discourse even though it may remain silent, unuttered" (p. 88).

Since discourse is dialogic and a sign is never a sign unless it is shared, meanings present a multiplicity within the exchange between the one and the other. Therefore, according to Bakhtinian theory, one's utterance (existence) is not solely controlled by discourse as an outside force because the intersubjectivity of the utterance makes room for multiaccentuality. From this perception of the intersubjectivity of the utterance (existence), human agents can struggle to overcome social domination.

The Bakhtinian theory of multifaceted/multiaccentuated language is opposed to, for instance, Foucault's (1972, 1977) or Derrida's (1976) pessimistic assumption that any kind of resistance cannot be considered a subversion of the dominant discursive paradigm, since this attempt to resist becomes influenced by the dominant discourse. Contrary to the Bakhtinian view, these postmodern theories neglect the potential influence of diverse voices within dialogic interaction as *modus operandi* for social agents' struggle. As Michael Gardiner (1992) remarks, "Foucault's rejection of subjectivity entails de facto acknowledgment that the enforcement of a dominant system of norms and 'disciplines' can never be resisted by an intersubjective, reflexive consciousness that could (at least potentially) be directed against the system" (p. 163). However, the major link between Bakhtinian and the postmodern theories is that both address the importance of considering history and culture as fundamental aspects to analyzing language.

A central aspect of Bakhtinian theory is to affirm the factors that connect all social signs to the larger cultural complexity in which these signs, such as language, constitute a purpose and become meaningful. In other words, there is no meaningfulness outside the contingencies of the culture because it is only within the cultural sphere that signs as well as people experience meaning. Voloshinov (1976) writes:

> Outside society and, consequently, outside objective socioeconomic conditions, there is no such thing as a human being. *Only as a part of a social whole, only in and through a social class, does the human person become historically real and culturally productive.* In order to enter into history it is not enough to be born physically. Animals are physically born but they do not enter into history. What is needed is, as it were, a second birth, a *social* birth. A human being is not born as an abstract biological organism but as a landowner or a peasant, as a bourgeois or a proletarian, and so on—that is the main thing. . . . *Only this social and historical localization makes him* [or her] *a real human being* and determines the content of his [or her] life and cultural creativity. [author's emphasis] (p. 15)

Therefore, the dialogic existence of both language and people is what establishes relations within the cultural-social-historical arena. The living dialogue among diverse social accentualities invites the creation of an arena in which diverse social interests and languages are not only existentially concrete but also crucial to the maintenance of human existence. In this sense, I agree with Richard Quantz and Terence O'Connor (1988), who brilliantly suggest that the Bakhtinian notion of the heteroglossic (multiaccentuality) and polyphonic essence of social life can be better understood through the concept of *multivoicedness.*

> [M]ultivoicedness seems to be a term that best captures the idea that any particular, concrete, historical dialogue is best described in terms of the multiple voices participating. . . . [T]he concept

of dialogue as a multivoiced social activity explains how the ideas of the powerful gain and maintain legitimacy as well as how the disempowered can attempt to legitimate their ideas and beliefs to others. Through the concepts of dialogue and multivoicedness Bakhtin offers us a framework for examining cultural continuity and change. (p. 99)

A dialogic existence represents a collective predicament toward social possibility, since consciousness has the potentiality of becoming conscious within the struggle for meaning. Here I mean that consciousness may perceive the community, the family, and the impact stemming from the contact with the other. However, for consciousness to become conscious, it is necessary to have not only an awareness of the self within the social group but, especially, an awareness of the ideological-social mechanisms that place people within relations of domination and subordination. For instance, a peasant may recognize her social condition/location as a peasant but may not recognize the reasons for this condition. A peasant may also recognize her family and the effects of the other within her life but may not recognize possible ways to overcome and change the constraints of her social condition. She may be able to discover ways of overcoming her position of social subordination only when her consciousness becomes conscious of the reasons/purposes for her struggle. As Richard Terdiman (1985) notes, "Purposiveness is conditioned by perception of a complex of concrete conditions in relation to which it is deployed" (p. 27). In this sense, Bakhtin argues that consciousness faces the necessity of choosing a specific kind of language. However, consciousness must be conscious of this ideological choice. Bakhtin writes an example of an illiterate peasant who lives miles away from an urban center and who lives immersed in diverse language systems; that is, this peasant prays, sings, and speaks to her family. For each of these situations, she utilizes a specific language system without knowing, without perceiving this passage from one to another system. However, as Bakhtin (1981) states,

as soon as it became clear that these were not only various different languages but even internally variegated languages, that the ideological systems and these languages contradicted each other and in no way could live in peace and quiet with one another—then the inviolability and predetermined quality of these languages came to an end, and the necessity of actively choosing one's orientation among them began. (p. 296)

In other words, the peasant is not conscious that she is inevitably engaged to an ideological choice within the multivoicedness of the world. From the Bakhtinian perspective, as soon as this peasant becomes conscious of this socio-ideological choice—conscious of her dialogic existence—she has the potential to overcome her subordinated position since she can perceive the ways in which the social structure affects and legitimates her own disempowerment.

Another example is that a student may recognize her lack of proficiency in a second language or she can also recognize the effects of this lack of proficiency within her relationships with teachers and other students. However, this student may not recognize the reasons for learning a second language since she is already "proficient" in her own language. Therefore, there exists a consciousness which is not conscious, since no one can struggle without knowing the reasons for the struggle. For instance, the explanation, "You must learn a language because you must learn a language" does not offer any room for non-English-speaking students to recognize the importance of learning a second language.

The struggle of social classes or the struggle to legitimate one's voice does not happen in a natural or unconstrained way. As Peter Hitchcock (1993) argues, "If dialogics become the celebration of the many-voicedness of language without showing the constraints on intersubjective exchanges, then they quite clearly fail as a paradigm of social formation" (p. 7). Therefore, consciousness becoming conscious is a process that reinforces the notion of the unstable and mutable existence of signs. This process also reinforces the notion that the struggle for meaning happens neither without a purpose nor spontaneously, just because people belong to diverse groups.

The struggle for meaning is the conflictual existence of dialogue. However, I believe this assumption has been neglected within the educational arena that perceives the students as passive individuals who must accept their "lessons" without questioning them.


## DIALOGIC PEDAGOGY

The Bakhtinian theory of dialogic existence is helpful to ground what I consider one of the major arguments of this study. The argument can be framed as follows: Since we cannot deny our dialogic existence, it seems obvious that one of the reasons for students' so-called "failure" in schools, especially in bilingual programs, is the lack of a dialogic pedagogy. It is only from this dialogic engagement that we can think not only of a bilingual but also of a multicultural education, in which diverse contextual meanings coexist. Such an engagement has the potential to critically transform reality.

Since we cannot think of social existence or language outside of dialogic interaction, I believe Paulo Freire's dialogic pedagogy offers an appropriate framework to illustrate the Bakhtinian assumption that consciousness has the critical potential of questioning and transforming existing ideologies. Since the first edition of the book *Pedagogy of the Oppressed*,[2] Paulo Freire gained recognition for advancing a revolutionary pedagogy. As Kathleen Weiler (1994) argues, "Paulo Freire is without question the most influential theorist of critical or liberatory education" (p. 13).

Despite the fact that the Brazilian educator Paulo Freire does not address his philosophy from the perspective of bilingual education, the dialogic pedagogy he advocates is appropriate to address the ways in which consciousness has the potential of becoming conscious within the social arena. As Thomas Oldenski (1994) summarizes, "The method of this pedagogy is one of dialogue or problem posing as opposed to a 'banking' methodology, valuing the voices and experiences of the students in the process of developing knowledge" (p. 47). Furthermore, the appropriateness of Freire's work to address the urgency of a dialogic pedagogy lies in the sense that the process of literacy is an endless as well as a social and political process. Following this idea, awareness is a key concept of Freire's pedagogy. As Michael Peters and Colin Lankshear (1994) note, "according to Freire's philosophy . . . human development is based upon a certain quality of awareness: awareness of our temporality, our 'situatedness' in history, and of our reality as being capable of transformation through action in collaboration with others. This is precisely to be critically conscious" (p. 181).

Paulo Freire does not mention the theories developed by the Bakhtin circle as a theoretical ground for his philosophy of education. However, I

---

2. *Pedagogy of the Oppressed* sold over 500,000 copies worldwide (Publisher's foreword, 1993). The first U.S. edition of this book was published in 1970.

believe a Freirean understanding of dialogue is closer to the Bakhtinian assumptions of language and consciousness than Lev Vygotsky's.[3]

There exists a myriad of similar epistemological assumptions addressed by Vygotsky and the Bakhtin circle. Both the Bakhtinian as well as the Vygotskian theories emphasize the crucial role of social factors in one's life. Both theories also argue that language consolidates the way in which we perceive the world. In other words, both theories advocate that consciousness is linked to the world of signs (language). Furthermore, both theories advocate that the process of thinking is never an isolated process since the other is always existent and, therefore, communication and thinking are dialogical in essence. However, Freire's dialogic pedagogy is closer to the Bakhtinian theory because he also perceives dialogue as offering a strong potential for questioning the dominant system. Freire as well as the Bakhtin circle believe that when consciousness becomes conscious of its social and historical location and its existential-social moment, then it has the potential to struggle toward the defense of its own meanings within the social arena. From this perspective, Paulo Freire argues that

> the dominant ideology 'lives' inside us and also controls society outside. If this domination inside and outside was complete, definitive, we could never think of social transformation. But, transformation is possible because consciousness is not a mirror of reality, not a mere reflection, but is reflexive and reflective of reality. (Shor and Freire, 1987, p. 13)

Despite the fact that Vygotsky's theory of consciousness is one in which "humans are viewed as constantly constructing their environment and their representations of this environment by engaging in various forms of activity" (Wertsch, 1985, p. 188), Bakhtinian as well as Freirean consciousness moves beyond some aspects of Vygotsky because, in the former two cases, consciousness has the socio-political potential to overcome the

---

3. Lev Semyonovitch Vygotsky 's (1896–1934) sociolinguistic theories challenge the psychological theories of Jean Piaget in that Vygotsky (1978) argues that human development is not uniform and identical purely based on biological stages; instead, he believes this development reflects interaction with social conditions and each individual consciousness is constructed through social relations with other people. Many scholars have related Freire's work to Vygostky's theory (e.g., Ira Shor and Paulo Freire, 1987; Nan Elsasser and Vera Steiner, 1987; Kyle Fiore and Nan Elsasser, 1987).

dominant sign. This conception of consciousness is one in which the social agents exist in a constant struggle for meaning. Therefore, both the Bakhtin circle and Paulo Freire perceive human existence within an incessant social struggle in which consciousness has the potential not only to address a social-contextual questioning of the existing situation but also to challenge this situation. In this way, the Bakhtinian theory of the dialogic existence justifies the urgency of the dialogic pedagogy addressed by Freire.

Recognizing that dialogue is itself creative and re-creative, Freire notes that dialogue

> must be understood as something taking part in the very historical nature of humans beings. . . . To the extent that we are communicative beings who communicate to each other as we become more able to transform our reality, we are able to know that we know, which is something more than just knowing. . . . In communicating among ourselves, in the process of knowing the reality which we transform, we communicate and know socially even though the process of communicating, knowing, changing, has an individual dimension. But the individual aspect is not enough to explain the process. Knowing is a social event with nevertheless an individual dimension. What is dialogue in this moment of communication, knowing and social transformation? Dialogue seals the relationship between the cognitive subjects, the subjects who know, and who try to know. (Shor and Freire, 1987, pp. 98–99)

Freire's theory of a dialogic pedagogy can be helpful for bilingual education because students are not perceived as individuals with empty minds who will learn a language. From the Freirean perspective, students and teachers enter into a critical and creative dimension within the teaching-learning process connected to their own existential experiences and cultural backgrounds. Both teachers and students critically perceive their realities and create knowledge within dialogue. The relevant aspect of Freire's pedagogy is its epistemological perspective within the process of creating knowledge; its relation to people's existential and cultural experiences; and its social dimension in the process of "conscientization." Therefore, I continuously recognize "the importance of Paulo Freire's work for establishing a condition of global possibility" (Moraes, 1992b, p. 129). Because of this hope of global possibility, I also believe the

Bakhtinian notion of dialogue can deepen not only Freire's dialogic pedagogy but also the social-political project of critical pedagogy. However, before the discussion of the ways in which the Bakhtinian theory can deepen Freire's theoretical assumptions toward a more "contextualized" bilingual education, it is necessary to discuss Freire's[4] theory within the U.S. educational arena.

## CRITICAL/RADICAL PEDAGOGY

Derived largely from Paulo Freire's work, a new movement called critical/radical pedagogy has emerged within the U.S. educational setting. Among many scholars who have been related to the growing movement of critical pedagogy, the names of Ira Shor, Peter McLaren, and Henry Giroux deserve special attention since these scholars, among others, introduced the work of Freire and continue to amplify his epistemological assumptions within the U.S. educational arena. At the present time, the work of these three scholars has crossed the frontiers of the United States and has been published throughout Europe and South America. To clarify the epistemological assumptions of critical pedagogy, I will mention the theories addressed by Peter McLaren and Henry Giroux .[5]

Critical pedagogy has been a revolutionary movement in the way we think about the meaning of education, teaching, and learning. Peter McLaren (1989) writes:

Critical pedagogy has begun to provide a radical theory and analysis of schooling, while annexing new advances in social theory and developing new categories of inquiry and new

---

4. For a broader and insightful understanding of Paulo Freire's philosophy and pedagogy see Paulo Freire's *Pedagogy of the Oppressed* (1993); Ira Shor and Paulo Freire's *A Pedagogy for Liberation: Dialogues on Transforming Education* (1987); Paulo Freire and Antonio Faundez's *Learning to Question* (1989); and Peter McLaren and Peter Leonard's (eds.) *Paulo Freire: A Critical Encounter* (1993).

5. U.S. feminist scholars have criticized critical/radical scholars such as Paulo Freire; Peter McLaren; Henry Giroux; and Ira Shor, arguing that critical pedagogy represents a master-narrative in which there is little room for the articulation of female voices. This existing critique is especially addressed by Carmen Luke and Jennifer Gore (1992); Jennifer Gore (1992); Elizabeth Ellsworth (1992); and Kathleen Weiler (1994).

methodologies. Critical pedagogy does not, however, constitute a homogeneous set of ideas. It is more accurate to say that critical theorists are united in their objectives: to empower the powerless and transform existing social inequalities and injustices. (p. 159)

Critical pedagogy is a pedagogy that affirms student voice and debate and renders citizens better able to act in the democratic process of transforming society. This means inquiry into self and society coupled with the ability to problematize all areas of study. The major goal of this pedagogy is to situate learning in students' experiences, cultures, present understanding, aspirations, and daily lives. The social and political project of critical pedagogy is the transformation of society through challenging dominant power relations and the ideologies that support them. Peter McLaren (1989) elucidates the challenge of critical theorists:

Especially within the last decade, critical educational theorists have come to view schooling as a resolutely political and cultural enterprise. Recent advances in the sociology of knowledge, cultural and symbolic anthropology, cultural Marxism, and semiotics have led these theorists to see schools not only as instructional sites, but also as cultural arenas where a heterogeneity of ideological and social forms often collide in an unremitting struggle for dominance. Within this context, critical theorists generally analyze schools in a twofold way: as sorting mechanisms in which select groups of students are favored on the basis of race, class, and gender; and as agencies for self and social empowerment. (p. 160)

Critical pedagogy both criticizes and extends the liberal ideology toward a more radical view of education, a view that problematizes knowledge as historically constructed and mediated by dominant interests and values. This analysis is mediated by critical thinking—the process by which consciousness becomes conscious of itself. (Of course, to be conscious is always to be *partially* conscious; consciousness can never be fully transparent to itself.) Critical pedagogy is a pedagogy with the political goal of creating a more just society instead of accommodating and adjusting students to the existing social setting. However, critical pedagogy has often been confused with the term *critical thinking* and the meaning of critical thinking has been differently used by liberals and neoconservatives, as Peter McLaren (1989) explains:

> Unfortunately, in their discussion of "critical thinking" the neo-conservatives and liberals have neutralized the term critical by repeated and imprecise usage, removing its political and cultural dimensions and laundering its analytic potency to mean "thinking skills." In their terms, teaching is reduced to helping students acquire high levels of cognitive skills. Little attention is paid to the purpose to which these skills are to be put. (p. 161)

Henry Giroux (1988b) addresses the distinction between liberal, conservative, and radical insights of education. This distinction is helpful in our understanding of critical pedagogy.

> [T]he *ultraconservatives* have constructed an unproblematic view of history in which it is argued that schools once acted as the moral gatekeepers of society. . . . The goal is to ensure that students take their rightful places in the social and occupational order. . . . It is a pedagogy marked by a rigid view of knowledge, an uncritical view of American history, and a refusal to develop a theory of learning in which students are allowed to speak from their own traditions and voices. . . . Teachers have also lost power through the standardization of school curricula, including the adoption by many school systems of prepackaged, so-called teacher-proof curricula. . . . The *liberal* faith in reason, science, and instrumental rationality has played a decisive role in shifting liberal discourse away from the politics of everyday life while simultaneously grounding its analyses in the celebration of procedural rather than substantive issues. . . . The complex relations of power along with the concrete problems of existing social and educational life in capitalist society often get lost in this work. . . . A *radical* theory . . . [rejects] this position as the starting point for developing a critical theory of education. Instead, educators should link a theory of ethics and morality to a politics in which community, difference, remembrance, and historical consciousness become foundational. . . . In effect, a major task for a critical theory of education is to analyze how historically constituted experiences of moral and political activ-

ity can contribute to developing an ethical discourse with an emancipatory political intent. [emphasis added] (pp. 42–58)

Therefore, critical pedagogy does not advocate a pre-defined body of knowledge that all students will be expected to learn because such a body of knowledge embraces the conservative, traditional goal of outcome-based learning. This single body of knowledge is, in fact, part of a management system that reduces the role of the teacher to that of a curator of materials.

From a critical perspective, language is used to legitimate one voice or history over another, and language does not only influence students toward a particular world view but also serves as a vehicle of alienation by preventing access to certain questions and answers. Furthermore, critical educational theorists believe power is not only visible in written and spoken language. The body itself is fully political and fully acted upon by forms of objectification and domination. Critical educational theorists argue that schools promote what is understood as "correct knowledge." The goal of the curriculum in schools is to convert students' wrong, distorted, or absent knowledge into an official knowledge, which is considered relevant and appropriate by the dominant ideology. From this conversion, a dichotomy of knowledge emerges. On the one hand, there exists the knowledge schools inculcate in students in order to produce servants for advantageous manipulation. On the other hand, there exists students' previous knowledge, which must be forgotten. The first knowledge is the dominant knowledge and the second is the knowledge that is subjugated. Therefore, according to critical educational theorists, only as we understand and help students to grasp the knowledge-power relationship do we recognize that knowledge might misrepresent social relations of privilege or reproduce the status quo. In other words, by situating schools in a political context, questions can be raised regarding the "hidden curriculum" embedded in the informal messages and practices produced by dominant pedagogical and curricular practices. Peter McLaren (1989) clarifies the way in which critical educational theorists perceive curriculum:

[T]he curriculum represents much more than a program of study, a classroom text, or a course syllabus. Rather, it represents the introduction to a particular form of life; it serves in part to prepare students for dominant or subordinate positions in the existing society. The curriculum favors certain forms of knowledge over others and affirms the dreams, desires, and values of select groups of students over other groups, often discriminatory on the basis of race, class, and gender. In general, critical educational theorists are concerned with how descriptions, discussions, and representations in textbooks, curriculum materials, course content, and social relations embodied in classroom practices benefit dominant groups and exclude subordinate ones. In this regard, they often refer to the hidden curriculum. . . . The hidden curriculum refers to the unintended outcomes of the schooling process. Critical educators recognize that schools shape students both through standardized learning situations, and through agendas including rules of conduct, classroom organization, and the informal pedagogical procedures used by teachers with specific groups of students. (p. 183)

The hidden curriculum and the power relationships it entails serve to act as conservative socializing forces on students instead of preparing them to understand society from critical perspectives, which will allow them to actively seek a reshaping of the world. Therefore, critical pedagogy stresses an active study of power, language, culture, and history. Furthermore, knowledge is examined for the ways in which it reflects the experiences of people.

In critical pedagogy, the curriculum is made meaningful because it includes important aspects of the students' everyday existence. Students are able to make a connection between their own experiences and the ongoing struggles in the social-political world and thereby work to alter oppressive conditions. In building the curriculum, teachers draw upon the experiences of the students. Students' voices are heard and taken into account. Both students and teachers have the authority to decide what kind of material will be utilized as part of the curriculum.

In critical pedagogy, the goal is not academic "excellence"—a buzz word that has been used everywhere to reinforce educational hierarchies of privilege—but rather the emancipation and empowerment of both students and teachers. It is important to understand that classroom pedagogical practice is viewed as strongly influenced by socio-political forces that bear down upon it in a myriad of ways. Therefore, according to critical pedagogy, a word, a sentence, an articulated discourse, do not materialize out of air; instead, they are viewed as historical and social constructions. For this reason, it is crucial that students and teachers can understand how schools are inscribed by discourses and practices of power that inform the larger society and cannot, therefore, operate independently of the society in which they exist. In this sense, being critical means being critically conscious. This is the main aspect of the liberatory education, as Freire remarks:

> Liberatory education is fundamentally a situation where the teacher and the students both have to be learners, both have to be cognitive subjects, in spite of being different. This for me is the first test of liberating education, for teachers and students both to be critical agents in the act of knowing . . . the context for transformation is not only the classroom but extends outside of it. The students and teachers will be undertaking a transformation that includes a context outside the classroom, if the process is a liberating one. (Shor and Freire, 1987, p. 33)

Critical educators encourage teachers and students to become agents in a struggle for social and political transformation. Solidarity among students and teachers takes the form of a counter-logic for social action. In other words, this counter-logic presents a terrain for appropriating meaning and experience and an opportunity for linking the political with the personal. Such a link also transcends the mind-body split and illustrates how power is mediated, resisted, and reproduced in everyday life. In this sense, teachers become what Giroux calls "transformative intellectuals" who make the pedagogical political and the political pedagogical by viewing schools as sites of struggle for meaning within a larger social project whereby students learn how praxis (critical reflection and action) can work to challenge social injustices. From this perception, hope and possibility enter into the picture when students are treated as critical agents and are not only given voice, but are affirmed in their own individual histories. Thus, as knowledge becomes not just something to be received as apolitical and ahistorical, but rather a problematic over which to struggle and contest, new meanings are produced.

## DIALOGIC-CRITICAL PEDAGOGY

As critical educational theorists argue, critical pedagogy's major project is that of empowering the powerless and transforming existing social inequalities. Therefore, for critical educational theorists, the relationship between oppressed and oppressors constitutes a key toward emancipation and liberation of the oppressed. However, critical educational theorists have been trapped in a constant search for a language that can significantly empower the oppressed. As Peter McLaren (1994c) notes, "Radical pedagogy must continue to search for a critical language that will stress the primacy of a politics of emancipation and interconnecting oppositional public spheres" (p. 198). At this point, the Bakhtinian theory of dialogue and dialogic existence can deepen the social and political project of critical and liberatory/emancipatory pedagogy addressed by critical educational theorists.

To develop a language adequate to such an emancipatory project, from the perspective of the Bakhtinian theory, there exists an urgent need to address the issue of the "pedagogy of the oppressor." By this, I mean that if we do not reinforce the relevance of a dialogic interaction between the oppressed and oppressor, it will be more difficult for the oppressed to overcome social constraints and, therefore, to be empowered. From this perspective, the awareness of the oppressed is fundamental, but the awareness of the oppressor is crucial in the sense that the oppressor can understand that he or she must collaborate for a better society, for his or her own emancipation as part of the social arena. If the oppressed and the oppressive consciousness has a chance of becoming conscious, both oppressed and oppressor can be engaged in a dialogue that will interconnect these two social-oppositional spheres. Then we can take a truly liberatory step toward emancipation and social freedom and a step toward democracy because the oppressive groups will be able to understand that oppression toward the other becomes their own imprisonment.

If we are talking about dialogic existence and if we focus our attention just around the oppressed, we lose the Bakhtinian notion of the whole social dimension. It is worth noting that, according to the dialogic Bakhtinian perspective, we do not have dialogue between parts but dialogue among the totality, among the whole. Both oppressed and oppressor must understand that our dialogic existence is something that cannot be denied. This means we have to address dialogically the idea that society does not function within a small part but rather as whole structure which comprises and embraces oppressed and oppressor. As Michael Gardiner (1992) points out,

> following Bakhtin, it has to be emphasized that the production, distribution and appropriation of ideological texts or discourses cannot be adequately conceptualized in terms of a such simple or linear relation, but only as a series of complex 'moments', each

with its own relative autonomy, and each mediating the other in important ways. . . . Thus, it is important to note that concrete subjects are always located in a complex of historically-situated social and cultural practices, and that the text or symbolic system per se represents only a subset of this wider constellation of institutions, practices and structures. (p. 150)

We need to construct a *dialogic-critical pedagogy* that takes as its founding objective a living dialogue between oppressed and oppressors from which both groups can understand the social constraints that impede an emancipatory democracy, experience different levels of oppression, and comprehend their shared responsibility. It is within such a dialogic-critical pedagogy that we can think about individual emancipation and also about collective social transformation.

Within a *dialogic-critical pedagogy*, both oppressed and oppressive groups must understand that science, art, religion, politics, and economy are examples of the visible expressions of ideology codified into particular constellations which create what we call, more extensively, the "world." Both groups must understand that we have a tendency of seeing this world as genuine. That is, we tend to forget that this world is just one possible interpretation and is essentially a discursive construction. Both oppressed and oppressive groups must understand that despite our attempts to define life, our definitions are always ideological. Therefore, both groups must comprehend that they can challenge and change this "ready-made" ideological world.

How can we conceptualize a pedagogy for the oppressor? How can we make the oppressor aware that society cannot function fairly while people just think in egocentric and binaristic terms of domination and subordination? The fact is the oppressor must also understand and be aware of social inequalities. What is at stake here is that we have to address a dialogic-critical pedagogy in which students who occupy the position of oppressors understand that the oppositional relationship between oppressor and oppressed is not a relationship that will guarantee social freedom or social hope. It is important that the oppressor recognizes that both social freedom and social hope can be reached through dialogic interaction.

When the Bakhtin circle addresses the multivoicedness of society, they are, in fact, arguing that no one can be excluded from the conflictual multivoicedness of the world. As Paul de Man (1989) notes, "The function of dialogism is to sustain and think through the radical exteriority or heterogeneity of one voice with regard to any other" (p. 109). Therefore, both the oppressed and the oppressor constitute this multivoicedness. From this view, we have to invite the oppressors to become further aware that there is no social future if mechanisms of oppression continue. We have to make the oppressor aware that everybody is oppressed at some level. The multivoicedness addressed by the Bakhtin circle confirms this argument. It is from this perception of the multivoicedness, that critical educational theorists should further develop a dialogic language of awareness.

For instance, in the case of a white homosexual upper-class female, we can perceive that in terms of her being white and upper class, this individual can be considered an oppressor. However, as a homosexual and female, this individual is oppressed on two different levels. In this sense, multivoicedness means we are placed within positions of subordination and domination, even if we belong to the oppressor's group, even if we belong to the economic elite.

Turning our attention to what could be considered a "perfect" portrait of the oppressor, I wish to consider the case of a white upper-class heterosexual male. Imagine hypothetically that this "perfect" example from the dominant/oppressive group is our student. From a dialogic-critical perspective, certain questions can be raised: How can this particular individual understand the oppression of the oppressed? How can someone who has never experienced—or experienced only in a very limited way—sexual, economic, racial oppression, and oppression by gender understand the social and political meaning of oppression? I would argue that, first of all, this student must understand the levels in which he is oppressed. Nevertheless, he will be able to understand oppression only if he has the chance of being engaged in a dialogic-critical pedagogy that will address the meaning of the existing conflictual multivoicedness in which he is located. This dialogic-critical pedagogy will also need to address diverse levels of oppression and the relevance of a truly democratic existence in which such multivoicedness has the potential of creating the conditions for social and political emancipation within a liberatory dialogue. From the standpoint of dialogic-critical pedagogy, this student who represents the "perfect" portrait of the dominant/oppressive group can understand that he is also oppressed because he lives under institutional control. He can understand that he exists within a system that shapes his own behavior and way of thinking. This is the awareness and critical consciousness that the students from the oppressive groups do not have.

To illustrate the lack of a critical consciousness of the oppressive group, the words of Peggy McIntosh (1989) are appropriate.

My schooling gave to me no training in seeing myself as an oppressor, as an unfairly advantaged person, or as a participant in a damaged culture. I was taught to see myself as an individual whose moral state depended on her moral will. My schooling followed the pattern my colleague Elizabeth Minnich has pointed out: whites are taught to think of their lives as morally neutral, normative, and average, and also ideal, so that when we work to benefit others, this is seen as work which allows "them" to be more like "us." (p. 10)

McIntosh underscores the idea that the dominant/oppressive group has been educated toward a continuous process of oppressing the oppressed. In other words, the dominant/oppressive group has been educated toward a tacit understanding that they are superior. Therefore, the oppressed can be best empowered if we also turn our attention to the oppressors. It seems contradictory but it is not. We need to create conditions for oppressors to critically analyze their own situation; to critically analyze the levels in which they are also oppressed because they live under various forms of social control and are discursively positioned in contradictory ways that blind them to their own situatedness in relations of power and privilege. Then students from the oppressive groups will be able to understand the oppression of the oppressed, since they are also part of the oppressed group that is ideologically controlled. This means a whole social awareness not only of students' own locations but also of their locations in relation to other locations. As Terence O'Connor and Richard Quantz (1991) remark, students who belong to the dominant/oppressive group must understand

the way in which they have been privileged yet dominated, promoted yet marginalized, advantaged yet disadvantaged. . . . [S]tudents cannot come to understand their subject positions outside public discussion with those positioned as Others; they can only learn how public discussion is advanced as they reconstruct their understanding of Others and Self in public dialogue. (p. 278)

From this perception, we can further emphasize social emancipation. We can also discuss counter-hegemonic forms of pedagogy toward the empowerment of the oppressed since the awareness of the oppressor is essential to the oppressed. From a dialogic-critical pedagogy, we can think of an engagement among multifaceted oppositional spheres in which differences are not a threat but necessary to perceive the ideological domain that obstructs social hope and freedom. As Pavel Medvedev (1978) appropriately articulates:

> When several people consume products, they remain separate entities as far as the process of consumption is concerned. But participation in the perception of an ideological product presupposes special social relationships. Here the very process is intrinsically social. Special forms of social intercourse are established for the plurality perceiving the ideological product. (p. 11)

It is not enough to recognize why there are so many people living in poverty while few people have everything; why women have not achieved equal pay for equal work, for instance. Within a dialogic-critical pedagogy, students from the oppressive groups cannot deny their own location as privileged individuals but the issue becomes how they can, as privileged people, be transformed into social agents who can change the existing social inequalities and ideologies that constrain their own existence; how they can, from a privileged social condition, help to construct a better society and avoid the naive consciousness of their own forthcoming generation.

## CONCLUSION

The Bakhtin circle argues that the dialogic existence of people and language is translated into a dialogic relationship in which the words of the speaker reaches the listener (who is another speaker). From the Bakhtinian theory of language and existence, dialogue is a coexistence in which speaker interacts with another speaker—a dialogue among contexts.

From the Freirean theory, existence is forged in dialogue. Dialogue is fundamental to social and political existence. Therefore, through the lenses of both theories, emerges a *dialogic-critical pedagogy* that makes the possibility for voices to be heard within a dialogic social awareness in which the voice of the oppressed reaches the oppressor (who is another oppressed)—and both agents must be engaged toward a reciprocal social freedom.

A dialogic-critical pedagogy can address a multivoiced emancipatory social hope in which the oppositional relationship of "oppressed *versus* oppressor" is transformed into a dialogic social existence of "oppressed *with* oppressed' (people who previously thought they could oppress without being oppressed or people who did not understand mechanisms of oppression). Following this view, students have the critical resources to analyze both their own and other groups and constantly question the prevailing values and beliefs of each.

# CHAPTER FIVE

# BILINGUAL ENCOUNTER: A DIALOGIC-CRITICAL PEDAGOGY

*But I do not wish to turn shortcomings into
virtues; in these works there is much external open-endedness not of the thought itself
but of its expression and exposition.
Sometimes it is difficult to separate one
open-endedness from another. . . .*
—Bakhtin (1986, p. 182)

In my discussion of bilingual education, I have tried to establish the
argument that dominant groups in U.S. society have been represented
through monolingual English-speaking people, while the oppressed people
constitute non-English speakers. However, the following question seems
relevant: Who has less proficiency:—those who know a second language
(although they still experience problems) or those who are monolingual?
From the perspective of a *dialogic-critical pedagogy*, the teaching of an
unquestionable monologic language and its abstract systems cannot be the
most important reason for the existence of bilingual education. This is the
main argument I wish to emphasize throughout this final chapter.

## BEYOND ENGLISH-PLUS VERSUS ENGLISH-ONLY: TOWARD THE LIVING DIALOGUE

Tamara Lucas, Rosemary Henze, and Ruben Donato (1990) elucidate what contributes to successful "language minority" high school stu-

dents in bilingual programs. The authors considered successful those schools which received formal recognition from state or federal agencies, and those which could provide quantitative evidence for success, such as dropout rates, daily students' attendance, and standardized test scores. The data for their study were collected at five schools in California and at one in Arizona and consisted of transcribed interviews (with school administrators, teachers, and students), questionnaires (for students), classroom observations, and program descriptions. The authors explain that "five of the six schools were relatively large, with 1,700 to 2,200 students. . . . Latino students constituted the largest single group—more than one-third of the school population" (p. 322). Lucas, Henze, and Donato (1990) address eight features that promoted successful students in bilingual programs at these six schools:

> [a] Value is placed on the students' languages and cultures . . .
> [b] High expectations of language-minority students are made concrete (they help students to achieve success) . . . [c] School leaders make the education of language-minority students a priority . . . [d] Staff development is explicitly designed to help teachers and other staff serve language-minority students more effectively . . . [e] A variety of courses and programs for language-minority students is offered . . . [f] A counseling program gives special attention to language-minority students . . . [g] Parents of language-minority students are encouraged to become involved in their children's education . . . [h] School staff members share a strong commitment to empower language-minority students through education. (pp. 322–335 )

Therefore, the mystery surrounding the education of minority students seems resolved. When there exists respect and understanding for diversity there exists commitment, achievement, and success, right? Wrong. Or, better to say—almost wrong. Respect for cultural diversity is relevant, relevant and fundamental, but that is not the end of the matter. What is no less important is the kind of leadership and educational policies that permeate a bilingual program. With respect to the school policies which were the focus of the study by Lucas, Henze, and Donato (1990), some aspects seem crucial for success. First, some of the school principals are able to hire the appropriate teachers; this means teachers who understand cultural diversity, who understand the community, and, if possible, who live in the community from where students come. Second, there are schools in which teachers receive an extra bonus in their salaries to acquire bilingual proficiency. Third, some counselors are Latinos and Latinas. Fourth, some schools promote periodic meetings among students, teachers, and parents to discuss curriculum activities. Fifth, minority-language students are not the minority, but a majority. All of these characteristics reflect political actions that help empower the development of groups considered minorities. Therefore, Lucas, Henze, and Donato (1990) illustrate the importance of appropriate educational policies as crucial aspects for successful bilingual programs. A policy based on a politics of pluralism and the participation of the community is essential for bilingual education.

Considering that the teaching-learning process occurs in a social and cultural context, a discussion of these contexts for bilingual education is of vital importance. The importance lies in the fact that this discussion extends the existing debate between English-plus and English-only, because it is not only focused on language acquisition but on the dialogical existence of individuals and language. Here, the theories addressed by the Bakhtin circle and Paulo Freire play a crucial role.

Usually, a lack of cultural awareness leads teachers to emphasize what their minority students cannot do or do not know, rather than what they can do or know. Another problem, no less relevant, is that the focus of language learning is always in English written expression. Furthermore, the problem in most classroom settings is that students have little chances of experiencing a dialogic pedagogy in which they can express their personal views from a critical perspective. The students' passive attitude brings to the pedagogical encounter a sense that students can talk only when they need to answer teachers' questions. From the perspective of such a passive attitude, students are not agents of their own learning process, because their forced passiveness becomes a territory of invisible existence. As Paulo Freire (1993) remarks, this passiveness is one of the major characteristics of a "banking education" in which

> the teacher teaches and the students are taught;
> the teacher knows everything and the students know nothing;
> the teacher thinks and the students are thought about;
> the teacher talks and the students listen—meekly;
> the teacher disciplines and the students are disciplined;
> the teacher chooses . . . and the students comply;
> the teacher acts and the students have the illusion of acting
>     through the action of the teacher;
> the teacher chooses the program content and the students (who
>     were not consulted) adapt to it. (p. 59)

The dominant perspective in bilingual education research reinforces what students do not know rather than what they can do. Yet, paradoxically, we expect teachers to reinforce students' self-esteem based on what students know. While progressive educational reform efforts have generally been against standardized tests, grammatical correctness, and so forth, the majority of educational research on bilingual education has emphasized evaluations of bilingual programs according to scores on standardized tests and on written material in general.

There exists little room for standardized tests within the conception of a dialogic-critical pedagogy for bilingual education, since these standards are not reflective of students' culture and daily experiences. Therefore, within a *dialogic-critical pedagogy*, ways of assessment must consider the progress of students based on the knowledge that students create in the classroom as well as the knowledge they bring to the classroom. In other words, these tests must consider the ways in which teachers and students develop the curriculum instead of reproducing the idea that "one size fits all." Furthermore, tests should consider and value what students know rather than betray an obsession for students' quantity of errors in second language, based on a hypothetical ideal speaker-hearer.

One aspect that seems clear within bilingual education is that there exists a distinction between the language learned in the classroom and the everyday use of language in pragmatic contexts. I am referring, in other words, to Chomsky's distinction between competence and performance. Therefore, context becomes something worthless as a second language is imposed on students. An obvious problem here is not the acquisition/acceptance of a second language but how this acquisition occurs in classrooms. Since it is impossible to acquire a second language outside of social constraints, the role of culture becomes an important focus of language acquisition. Thus, I wish to turn our attention toward a formulation of possible ways to transform bilingual education from a monologic into a dialogic existence. In this sense, I think the monologic process of a learning-teaching process simply based on an acquisition of a specific language has shown its inconsistent outcomes, because language is considered an abstraction to be learned while students' previous speaking consciousness is rarely considered.

The notion that teachers are responsible for students' achievement in bilingual programs is visibly present within the research community (Edmonds, 1979; Cummins, 1991). Considering teachers have a crucial role within the teaching-learning process, some scholars have emphasized teachers' major problems in bilingual programs as follows: Teachers do not want changes in the curriculum (Reyes, 1992); they do not have a sympathetic interaction with students who do not speak English (Nieto, 1993); many of them are opposed to bilingual programs (Otheguy, 1991); they have the power to empower students as well as to transform them into politically disabled people (Cummins, 1991); they are not bilingual speakers (Ada, 1986), and they just use standardized tests in their teaching (Sleeter and Grant, 1988). Although I recognize and agree with the importance and responsibility of teachers who work in bilingual programs, I believe some characteristics of the teacher's role must be developed formulating a dialogic-critical pedagogy for bilingual education.

To work successfully with cultural diversity in classrooms, teachers need to have more than an attitude of respect for this diversity. Teachers must also understand their students in the light of the community in which they live, instead of understanding students' behavior as unacceptable deviations from specific dominant norms. Peter McLaren appropriately remarks that "for too many minorities, schools have become Cathedrals of Death, agencies for reintegration, camps for ideological internment, factories for domestication" (Steinberg, 1992, p. 398). In this sense, non-English-speaking students are penalized in the school system because the values, attitudes, and behavior—the "cultural capital"—of the English-speaking people are reinforced and rewarded. However, the mere recognition of this form of oppression is, of course, too simplistic to serve as the support for a dialogic-critical pedagogy. The important issue is, beyond such a recognition, a commitment to change this mechanism of oppression. As a matter of fact, the school structure generally mirrors and repeatedly communicates lasting norms, basic assumptions, and models of human interaction as part of the hidden curriculum. As part of the hidden curriculum, schools reproduce the hierarchical order in society.

The benefits of recognizing schools as cultural zones of contest and as sites of domination cannot be denied. This is exactly one of the major contributions of critical educational theorists. On the other hand, there exists another necessary step; educators and theorists alike may come to realize the need for a theory that accounts for potential varieties of resistance. In this sense, Bakhtinian perspectives offer the necessary explanatory ground for articulating such modes of resistance so the complexities of the social multivoicedness can be better analyzed. For instance, Michael Gardiner argues that contemporary postmodern thought does not properly address the potential for resistance and argues instead for a Bakhtinian analysis. Gardiner (1992) emphasizes that

> Bakhtin's critical strategy is not just to demonstrate the conventional architectonics of discourse. He also wants to show that texts can be re-constructed or discursively re-ordered, be made to produce very different meanings through recontextualization, the juxtaposition of different narratives or texts, and so on. . . . Bakhtin conceives of the subversion of monologic discourse as taking the form of a peculiar kind of deconstructive tradition which is enacted by the people, one that . . . breaks the fetters of the old world. . . . What this implies . . . is that the 'self' for Bakhtin is not constituted through a unified, monadic relation to the external world; rather, the phenomenon of 'self-ness' is constituted through the operation of a dense and conflicting network of discourses, cultural and social practices and institutional structures, which are themselves bound up with the intricate phenomenology of the self-other relation. And since this process is fundamentally historical and not a singular 'event', it is continuous and 'mobile'. (pp. 164–165)

Therefore, it is important for the teaching-learning process that teachers can recognize how and why mechanisms of resistance are constructed, not only by students but also by themselves. Despite their location within a particular social class or ethnic group, students and teachers act out constantly against a multiplicity of forces; resistance is not only undertaken by a "subordinate" culture. However, it is worth noting that in our capitalist society economically disenfranchised students experience higher levels of social oppression, this oppression is increased when they happen to be female or non-white students. In this sense, mechanisms of resistance often become more visible. The problem is that in most classroom settings mechanisms of resistance are very often considered by teachers as a "rebellion without a real cause," instead of a response to a monologic discourse, in Bakhtinian terms, that denies students' lived experiences. In fact, resistance is a confrontation between social backgrounds and a symbolic resource against the monologic discourse. Nevertheless, this limited interpretation by teachers constitutes part of a dominant ideology that helps reproduce asymmetrical relations of power. In this sense, I agree with William Kennedy (1987) when he remarks that "resistance to the reproductive continuity of the dominant ideology motivates transformative education . . . [and] inadequate analysis lets people focus on the surface of things rather than on the deeper connections and assumptions" (pp. 238–239).

The major reason for the lack of teachers' cultural and social awareness is explained by Donaldo Macedo (1993), who argues that "courses such as race relations, ethics, and ideology are almost absent from the teacher preparation curriculum. This serious omission is, by its very nature, ideological, and constitutes the foundation for what I call the pedagogy of big lies" (p. 186).

Opposed to an alienating pedagogy, Alma Ada (1986) suggests a teacher-training process based on a critique of bilingual education. She argues that "in many instances they themselves [teachers] have been victims of language oppression and racism; thus, in order to empower their students to overcome conditions of domination and oppression, they must first be empowered themselves" (p.386). Basing her pedagogy on Paulo Freire's philosophy, Ada (1986) discussed with teachers their own roles as teachers and as people who socially construct society, as well as the problems they face in everyday school life. The basic focus of Ada's group discussions was an evaluation of teacher education programs. One of the teachers involved in Ada's group discussion said: "They preached to us to teach creatively, but we were never allowed any creativity. They encouraged us to be good communicators, but the classes they taught were deadly. There was some lip service paid to the need for encouraging children to think, but we were expected to memorize and repeat" (p. 393). Ada (1986) reports that after class discussions all of the groups involved began to consider teaching as a political act and addressed powerlessness as the major problem they faced.

Among the many mistakes of teacher education programs, one problem needs to be highlighted: Teachers learn that one kind of methodology is good for all students. Maria Reyes (1992) explains that this way of thinking is incompatible for any kind of dialogical learning, especially within bilingual programs. On the basis of her findings from a case study in a fourth-grade bilingual classroom in Colorado, Reyes (1992) states that the following factors contribute to successful teaching for students who are "linguistically different:"

a) the organization of a cooperative learning classroom where assisting others in completing academic tasks was more important than individual competition;
b) the provision of explicit skills instruction within the context of learning activities and, without hesitation, to cite individual errors in a culturally sensitive manner;
c) heterogeneous grouping of students by language and ability so that students could learn both content and a second language from each other; and
d) use of Spanish and English literature books, supported by mediation of LEP students' reading comprehension to help them make relevant connections to universal themes. (p. 442)

Furthermore, Reyes (1992) notes that the demand for a teacher to be bilingual is rarely presented as crucial. Although she recognizes that bilingual teachers are decidedly helpful, she mentions the case of a teacher who collaborated in the success of her Korean student without knowing any Korean words or expressions, but who encouraged this girl to always write in her own language. This teacher employed translators for the student's work and later this preliminary attitude was helpful for the student's acquisition of English.

One of the most relevant issues of bilingual education is sensitive educational decision making. In other words, these decisions are not limited to how much of the subject matter is covered in the classroom but how much time must be spent to allow students to be not only proficient in a second language but also aware of new cultural perspectives. For instance, Jim Cummins (1984) argues that courses of English as Second Language (ESL) are not sufficient because non-English-speaking students need at least five years to develop the necessary proficiency to function in monolingual English classes. In this sense, I agree with Cummins's (1993) perspectives: that ESL students do not feel confidence to express their views in an ESL classroom that is focused on transmitting second language skills without considering the ways in which students' cultural backgrounds, daily experiences, and interests affect their learning process.

It is crucial to consider the linguistic community. Here, I mean that it is necessary to know if the community is just bilingual or if it is multilingual without forgetting the peculiarities of a community. We need to remember the perspective of Bakhtinian multivoicedness, which maintains that people are not homogeneous even if they belong to a certain ethnic group. Therefore, a key issue becomes that of finding ways of working within a cross-cultural classroom. However, a basic assumption underlying a cross-cultural classroom is teachers should understand students learn better from social practices that have direct relevance to the materiality of their everyday lives.

The major contribution of Bakhtinian theory is a broader comprehension of the ways in which diversity plays a crucial role within the construction of social identities. Bakhtinian theory goes beyond the liberal view of celebration of pluralism to a more radical understanding of the effects of this plurality within the social arena. Therefore, the main issue is not to have "respect" for the marginalized or oppressed, as if this so-called respect was enough to empower the powerless, but, above all, to understand that the marginalized constitutes an active and essential part of their own social construction and that of the oppressor. As Robert Stam (1989) points out,

> any act of verbal or cultural exchange, for Bakhtin, leaves both interlocutors changed. The historical dialogue between blacks [sic] and whites in North America, for example, has profoundly changed both parties. Even white racists are not untouched by black [sic] culture. . . . Official America seems reluctant to recognize the extent to which it has been Africanized, although Africanization is everywhere evident. . . . Polyphony does not consist in the mere appearance of a representative of a given group, but in the fostering of a textual setting where that group's voice can be heard with its full force and resonance. (p. 131)

Of course, while Stam (1989) is correct, we need to remember the conditions in which dialogue takes place is not equal and the classroom is hardly the place where we find true reciprocity. Voices exist, but as part of a structured hierarchy in which whites set the conditions for the dialogue by defining what knowledge is valued and why. In this sense, Bakhtinian polyphony addresses the ways in which oppressed groups influence dominant groups and, therefore, have a latent potential to overcome their oppressive social situation. Bakhtin (1981) emphasizes that two individuals are mutually influenced by their discourses. One's discourse enters into the context of the other's discourse, and both individuals become linked within a dialogized context that cannot be denied. Within this dialogic interaction, the influence of one discourse over the other can be immense and inevitable. It is within this dialogic interaction between two individuals that these two contexts reach the climax of their existence, because individuals face each other's contexts and also the contexts of themselves.

One practice that is almost nonexistent in classrooms is the question-answer within student-student interaction. Usually, questions stem from teachers and students respond to teachers and not to other students. The classroom is, therefore, a space where students experience a pseudo-dialogical interaction. In fact, students rarely share their own views, the reasons for their learning process, or the existing variety of experiences they have in their communities. Unfortunately, students have little room to create a desire for learning. On the other hand, when teachers are engaged in a dialogic-critical pedagogy they recognize that interaction among students is fundamental. First, because a dialogic-critical pedagogy, does not neglect the students' dialogic existence (existence through the lenses of the other). Second, because a dialogic-critical pedagogy embraces the view that individuals do not become themselves unless they can live in dialogue.

Through a dialogic-critical pedagogy, it is possible to discuss with students the importance of knowing more than one language: Why should we become bilingual speakers? Why should we know about diverse cultures? What is the meaning of knowing someone else's culture and cultural background? Why should we know about the other? Within a dialogic-critical pedagogy students should discuss and explore the importance of being bilingual in the direction of a broader and more critical understanding of the world. Following this perspective, students and teachers should discuss the social contribution of people who know more than one language. The issue becomes a discussion of the ways in which both non-English-speaking and English-speaking students can work together to learn not only a second language but to learn from the perspectives of cultural diversity. Everybody can be committed within the learning process and further discuss inequalities within the existing social juxtaposition.

The primary question "Why should I learn a second language?" seems neglected in bilingual education programs. However, this question should be answered not only by non-English speakers but also by English-speaking students. Collective social awareness is an important step from which students can learn and grow in their perspectives. In this sense, a cooperative classroom is relevant because it is a way to awaken collective awareness and promote new cultural visions. Furthermore, cultural awareness represents diverse perceptions of the ways in which others experience society. This notion of social commitment among students is an important aspect that very often has been left behind. A group of students must be committed to their own success as a group and not as separate students. This commitment is clearly a counter-logic of capitalist domination in which both competition and possessive individualism obstruct any kind of participatory democracy. Therefore, students should feel their group is going to become determined to learn. Everybody can help everybody overcome difficulties. This sense of group commitment can be a strong weapon on the path to learning.

Despite the fact that a dialogic-critical pedagogy for bilingual education means a re-evaluation of programs and ways of assessment, two-way and maintenance bilingual programs seem to be closer to the needs of the development of a dialogic-critical pedagogy. In this sense, both groups—English and non-English speakers—might experience the process of acquiring a second language and have access to other cultures. Both groups might be engaged within a process of creating knowledge considering their cultural backgrounds and daily experiences. Within this perspective, both groups might perceive that their "differences" are relevant to the whole process of learning and social awareness.

Why is the word *difference* used to refer to cultural diversity? Personally, I completely reject the notion of "culturally different" because the word *different* carries connotations of opposite, unlike, contrary, divergent, and so forth. Rather, I prefer the word *diversity*. The word *different* has been used to specify an individual or a group of people who do not belong to a particular model of culture or language and, therefore, are different. From this perception, I agree with Joan Scott (1992) when she remarks that

> difference and the salience of different identities are produced by discrimination, a process that establishes the superiority or the typicality or the universality of some in terms of the inferiority or atypicality or particularity of others. . . . Administrators have hired psychological consulting firms to hold diversity workshops which teach that conflict resolution is a negotiation between dissatisfied individuals. Disciplinary codes that punish 'hate-speech' justify prohibitions in terms of the protection of individuals from abuse by other individuals, not in terms of the protection of members of historically mistreated groups from discrimination, nor in terms of the ways language is used to construct and reproduce asymmetries of power. (pp. 14–17)

Thus, it is necessary to continuously expand the perspective of the meaning of difference. As Peter McLaren (1993c) remarks, "Differences are always differences in relation, they are never simply free-floating. Differences are not seen as absolute, irreducible or intractable, but rather as undecidable and socially and culturally relational" (p. 113). The problem exists in mainstream educational research, especially in bilingual education: The words different and difference have been used, often unwittingly, from the viewpoint of the white Anglo majority population to indicate that a student or a group of students (non-English speakers, for instance) is 'deviant'. The absurdity of such a belief is illustrated by Jim Cummins (in press a) who remarks that

> a recent example of how persistent some of these linguistic prejudices are among academics who know little about language comes from a monograph on Latino/Latina children written by Lloyd Dunn (1987)[1]. . . . In expressing his concerns that bilingual education could result in "at least the partial disintegration of the United States of America" (pp. 66–67), Dunn argues that Latino/Latina children and adults "speak inferior Spanish" and that "Latin pupils on the U.S. mainland, as a group, are inadequate bilinguals. They simply don't understand either English or Spanish well enough to function adequately in school" (p. 49). . . . He attributes the causes of this lower scholastic ability about equally to environmental factors and 'to genes that influence scholastic aptitude'. (p. 64)

From a dialogic-critical perspective, we cannot simply assume that identities exist in isolation from each other. Diverse identities also coexist within the same historical and social arena. Therefore, we need to recognize that we do not have entirely separated histories but that we are part of the ceaseless construction of social existence. Furthermore, social multivoicedness rejects the assumption that, for instance, we just need to respect differences as if difference was not established through relational processes. Such "respect" represents the most conservative perspective on

---

1. Dunn, L. (1987). *Bilingual Hispanic Children on the U.S. Mainland: A Review of Research on Their Cognitive, Linguistic, and Scholastic Development.* Circle Pines: American Guidance Service.

social multivoicedness, since diversity does not exist separately but actively participates within social construction. As Richard Quantz and Terence O'Connor (1988) remark, "Society must be understood as in continuous dialogue and, therefore, multivoiced and nonconsensual" (p. 99). For this reason, I wish to emphasize that recognition and respect for human "differences" are not sufficient to guarantee multicultural education. As Antonia Darder (1991) points out,

> many situations exist in which students are presented with games, food, stories, language, music, and other cultural forms in such a way as to strip these expressions of intent by reducing them to mere objects disembodied from their cultural meaning. In order to prevent such an outcome, educators must become more critical not only of the actual curriculum they bring into the classroom, but also of the philosophical beliefs that inform their practice. (p. 113)

Schooling must be a daily practice of reflections and evaluations upon ourselves and our lives within the social system. Curriculum planners need to analyze what is going on beyond the classroom and assess the various needs of students. This means bilingual curriculum should involve contact not only with teachers and students but, especially, with members of the community. This view of curriculum is opposed to a prescribed curriculum in which the teacher is merely a classroom manager whose duty it is to get prescribed content across to students. A dialogic-critical pedagogy perceives students as dynamic and active people who are growing in perspectives within the construction of knowledge. As Bakhtin (1986) remarks, "The person who understands must not reject the possibility of changing or even abandoning his [or her] already prepared viewpoints and positions. In the act of understanding a struggle occurs, which results in mutual change and enrichment" (p. 181).

In the beginning of chapter 2 of this book, I argued that bilingual education does not have a conclusive definition. However, bilingual education is usually connected to the idea of simply acquiring a second language. This misunderstanding is so strong that studies in bilingual education have been developed to locate the level of second language proficiency. This constitutes one of the major educational mistakes of this field. If the acquisition of a second language is the only outcome of bilingual programs it should be called 'English instruction' and not 'bilingual education'. As we have seen in this book, from the perspective of a dialogic-critical pedagogy, bilingual education cannot be summarized as language acquisition because language is part of the whole cultural-ideological process in which social agents exist. Following this perspective, I agree with Michael Gardiner (1992) when he argues that

> ideological meaning is radically contextual in nature. . . . [T]he contextual significance of texts must be on the agenda of a critical theory of ideology as much as the mechanisms of significa-tion as such. This 'thesis of contextualization' constitutes a powerful prophylactic against the structuralist insistence on the absolute autonomy of discourse, and upon the supposition that 'ideology' is a certain kind or 'level' of signification. . . . Hence, ideology in Bakhtinian terms refers to the primary symbolic-linguistic medium through which individuals gain an awareness of their socio-historical situation and engage in struggle over scarce cultural, political, and economic resources. (p. 151)

There exists no language outside social and cultural relations. Therefore, the meaning of bilingual education must be strongly connected to bicultural education. In this sense, Bakhtinian and Freirean theories offer the necessary ground for teachers and curriculum planners to think about a contextualized multilingual-multicultural education. This, how-ever, does not mean these theories can be transformed into a recipe to be applied in all bilingual education classes, because each group of students (and teachers) have a myriad of living contexts from which they bring their own responsive understanding and meanings to daily activities in school. Furthermore, each student (and teacher) has a different history regarding the ways of 'becoming' a self and 'naming' the world. *A recipe for teaching and learning erases identities and contexts.* Definitely, one size does not fit all.

## CONCLUDING REMARKS

One of the primary assumptions of Marxian theory is that the aware-ness of social reality is also its change. In other words, once individuals become aware of their social condition and their relation with others, social reality changes. In this sense, knowledge is not an end in itself but a possibility for praxis. Praxis, from a Marxian perspective, transforms individuals because they are afforded a recognition of existing contradictions in social life. Therefore, the first step toward any form of social emancipation occurs when individuals leave their position of social alienation. In this sense, identity plays a crucial role.

As we have seen, identity is the social result of the contact we have with others. It is from the orientation of the other that we construct our identities. Therefore, our identity is not completely ours but lies on the edge of ourselves and the social arena. Social transformation implies a process of transforming identities.

As I stated in chapter 4 of this book, if we are searching for a critical emancipatory social transformation, changes in the relationship between oppressed and oppressive groups are necessary. For the purposes of such a transformation, a dialogic-critical pedagogy informed by the epistemological assumptions of the Bakhtin circle and Paulo Freire offers an insightful contribution toward the development of a politics of identity necessary for this transformation.

I agree with Abdul Janmohamed (1994) when he remarks that Paulo Freire's pedagogy offers students the possibility of agency. As Janmohamed (1994) emphasizes, by engaging students in a process of decodification and in advocating that the oppressed understand themselves as the 'antithesis' of the dominant group, "Freire implies a simultaneous transgression of one border and the establishment of another" (p. 249). From this perspective, students do not see the social world as natural but as human social construction. From a Freirean perspective, students perceive what was previously unperceivable and open a space for nascent identities. Freire addresses the courage to cross barriers of oppressive existence from which emerges a new identity that is aware of its own social, historical, and political location. This nascent identity is not a rejection of the previous identity but a constitution of a modified identity which perceives the importance of its own social location and its own potential for social transformation.

Both Freirean and Bakhtinian theories address the contingencies of transformation. Both Freire and the Bakhtin circle assert that domination is never complete but only partial. Furthermore, both theories advocate that collective awareness is fundamental to overcoming domination. As Voloshinov (1976) points out,

> in becoming aware of myself, I attempt to look at myself, as it were, through the eyes of another person, another representative

of my social group, my class. Thus, self-consciousness, in the final analysis leads us to class consciousness, the reflection and specification of which it is in all its fundamental and essential respects. (p. 87)

Despite the fact that Freire and the Bakhtin circle perceive dialogue in different ways, both theories, if taken together, offer an insightful perception of dialogue as a means of shaping existence toward social transformation. In other words, while Freire perceives dialogue as a helpful way to challenge social and ideological constructions used to oppress a social self, the Bakhtinian notion of dialogue is one which not only justifies existence but is also the meaning of our existence.

A Bakhtinian notion of dialogue is connected to the idea of dialogic relationships. There is no external dialogue if there is no internal dialogue, because the world exists from a dialogic perspective. As we have seen in previous chapters of this book, otherness is a crucial aspect of existence. In other words, *we live dialogically and language does not exist outside of dialogic existence.* Language, as well as existence, is forged in dialogic relations. As Bakhtin (1984) points out, "Language lives only in the dialogic interaction of those who make use of it. Dialogic interaction is indeed the authentic sphere where language lives" (p. 183).

A Freirean concept of dialogue is one in which consciousness has room for social self-reflection, questioning knowledge and life. Dialogue is part of a process of moving toward equal rights and of having sociopolitical voices. In other words, Freire's dialogue is forged in social participation of awareness within a process of transforming praxis (reflection and action). As Freire (1993) remarks, "Dialogue cannot occur between those who want to name the world and those who do not want this naming—between those who deny other men [and women] the right to speak their word and those whose right to speak has been denied them. . . . Dialogue is thus an existential necessity" (p. 71).

However, despite their differences, both Bakhtinian and Freirean analyses of dialogue call our attention to the fact that consciousness is a socio-ideological construction; that is, consciousness is not something that was biologically born within us. Both theories perceive consciousness as social. It is exactly within the construction of consciousness that language has a fundamental relevance: We exist within a process of absorbing other's words, especially because words are used to tell us who we are—a preconceived political location that shapes our identities.

Considering that the center represents the dominant/oppressive group and that the margins represent oppressed groups, both Paulo Freire and the Bakhtin circle address crucial strategic movements of awareness. These movements open a broader understanding for a politics of identity in which individual existence is a social event of conflicting parts. A Freirean movement would be *from the margins to the center*. A Bakhtinian movement would be *from the margins and from the center*. While Freire speaks from the perspective of changes in oppressed groups and addresses the borderline *between* oppressed and oppressive groups, the Bakhtin circle speaks from the perspective of changes in *both groups*, since no one can deny the dialogue of social multivoicedness. In this sense, both groups are socially interconnected and continuously affect each other. This does not mean, however, that Bakhtinian theory denies the existence of social domination and subordination. What is at stake here is that both oppressed and oppressive groups must be aware of their mutual situatedness within ideological formations and social relations. As Robert Stam (1989) points out, "Rather than a hierarchical base/superstructure model, Bakhtin presents the mediation between the two as a series of concentric circles, constantly rippling in and out, each with its own dynamism and specificity" (p. 120).

These strategic movements addressed by Paulo Freire and the Bakhtin circle are expanded and deepened within a reflexive consciousness that does not understand society as naive peaceful plurality but as conflictual coexistence. However, Bakhtin remarks that we need to leave the narrow sense of language as a unitary myth because a radical social revolution needs a total liberation from hegemonic intentions. These hegemonic intentions represent the major cause of keeping language (existence) as something unquestionable and immutable: "It is necessary that heteroglossia wash over a culture's awareness of itself and its language, penetrate to its core, relativize the primary language system underlying its ideology and deprive it of its naive absence of conflict" (Bakhtin, 1981, p. 368).

I would like to conclude by addressing some questions I consider relevant for discussing bilingual education in terms of constructing the beginnings of a dialogic-critical pedagogy: What are the ways in which non-English-speaking students construct meaning in bilingual classes? What is their opinion of the bilingual programs in which they are enrolled? How do these students justify their L2 learning? How do they interpret their experiences in classrooms? How do these students shape their own development as a form of resistance? What are the circumstances in which this resistance becomes more visible? How do English-speaking students perceive their non-English-speaking classmates? How do non-English-speaking students perceive their English-speaking classmates?

The above questions are important because they provide a closer examination of some of the complexities that very often are neglected within bilingual education classes and research, such as the primordial perception of our dialogic existence—*the perception of the "I" and the "other," simultaneously*. Furthermore, these questions address students' perception of their own learning-teaching processes connected to the location of their own identities within *the process of "becoming," which is forged in dialogue*. In this way, teachers as well as researchers may understand (through contextual lenses) the levels of development that students experience in the process of acquiring a second language.

An important issue surrounding bilingual programs can be summarized by the question: Who would be privileged with a bilingual program? "Everybody" would be a reasonable answer. Bilingual education does not mean transforming someone who knows two languages (even with problems in L2) into a monolingual individual. Bilingual education does not mean erasing meanings and knowledges. Bilingual education should not be understood as a substitution of frontiers, but rather access to diverse frontiers. Bilingual education should have a twofold development: English speakers could learn Spanish and Spanish speakers could learn English, for instance. This means bilingual programs should be addressed for both English and non-English speakers. Bilingual education is necessary for everybody. In this sense, non-English-speaking students might understand that they are also needed in classrooms because they can help English-speaking students to understand diverse cultures. Therefore, non-English-speaking students will not see themselves as disabled because difficulties of acquiring a second language becomes not a problem but a necessary and positive challenge for both groups of students as well as for teachers.

Bilingual programs should consider, first of all, multicultural history and social location. On the one hand, bilingual education separated from multicultural education means acquiring a language without social context; this represents a truncated and distorted understanding of language acquisition. On the other hand, a dialogic-critical pedagogy represents a possibility for a multicultural education that must address a politics of identity. This politics of identity must be seen as one in which diversity is a conflictual coexistence of plural identities within the social arena.

Because of the historical context in which bilingual programs began in the United States, it is common that one understands bilingual education as something only addressed to "minorities" and that it is, therefore, nonessential for everyone. Jim Cummins (in press b) emphasizes that

> culturally-diverse students are defined as deficient and confined to remedial programs that act to produce the deficits they were ostensibly intended to reverse. . . . Maintenance of the lies of history and the facade of equity requires that bilingualism continue to be defined as part of the problem rather than as part of the solution.

However, if educators and the general public can understand that bilingual and multicultural education offer possibilities for a renewed understanding of both the word and the world (Paulo Freire's perspective), perhaps schools can be seen as vital sites for the construction of a culturally and linguistically literate citizenry in which the dialogic existence of social multivoicedness (Bakhtinian perspective) plays a crucial role. For these reasons, I believe what hinders the development of bilingual and multicultural education is the hegemonic and monologic discourse of "helping minorities." As Dennis Carlson (1993b) exemplifies,

> in mostly-White, middle class suburbs, multicultural education often can hardly be said to be practiced at all, aside from formal recognition of African American history month or Martin Luther King's birthday. This reinforces a belief that multicultural education is for minority students and that other students do not need it since "their" (White, middle class) culture is already represented in the curriculum. (p. 13)

There is no place for any kind of supremacy in any country.

# REFERENCES

Abella, R. (1992). Achievement tests and elementary ESOL exit criteria: An evaluation. *Educational Evaluation and Policy Analysis*, 14 (2), pp. 169–174.

Abraham, R. (1983). Relationship between use of the strategy of monitoring and cognitive style. *Studies in Second Language Acquisition*, 6, pp. 17–32.

Ada, A. (1986). Creative education for bilingual teachers. *Harvard Educational Review*, 56 (4), pp. 386–394.

Ambert, A. and Melendez, S. (1985). *Bilingual Education: A Sourcebook*. New York and London: Garland.

August, D. and Garcia, E. (1988). *Language Minority Education in the United States: Research, Policy and Practice*. Springfield: Charles Thomas.

Back, E. (1987). *Fracasso do Ensino de Português: Proposta de Solução*. Petrópolis: Vozes.

Baker, K. and Kanter, A. (1983) (Eds.). *Bilingual Education: A Reappraisal of Federal Policy*. Lexington and Toronto: Lexington Books.

Bakhtin, M. (1981). *The Dialogic Imagination* (Caryl Emerson and Michael Holquist, Trans.). Austin and London: University of Texas Press.

Bakhtin, M. (1984). *Problems of Dostoevsky's Poetics* (Caryl Emerson, Trans.). Minneapolis: University of Minnesota Press.

Bakhtin, M. (1986). Notes 1970–1971. In Gary Morson (Ed.) *Bakhtin: Essays and Dialogues on His Work* pp. 179-182. Chicago and London: University of Chicago Press.

Bally, C. and Sechehaye, A. (1959). Preface. In Charles Bally and Albert Sechehaye (Eds.) *Course in General Linguistics* (W. Baskin, Trans.), pp. xiii–xvi. New York: Philosophical Library.

Barnes, R. (1983). The size of the eligible language-minority population. In Keith Baker and Adriana Kanter (Eds.) *Bilingual Education: A Reappraisal of Federal Policy*, pp. 3–32. Lexington and Toronto: Lexington Books.

Bhabha, Homi K. (1994). *The Location of Culture*. London and New York: Routledge.

Caramazza, A., Yeni-Komshian, G., Zurif, E., and Carbone, E. (1973). The acquisition of a new phonological contrast: The case of stop consonants in French-English bilinguals. *Journal of the Acoustical Society of America*, 54, pp. 421-428.

Cardenas, J. (1977). Response I. In Noel Epstein *Language, ethnicity, and the schools: Policy alternatives for bilingual-bicultural education.* Washington, D.C.: The Institute for Educational Leadership.

Carlson, D. (1993a). Literacy and urban school reform: Beyond vulgar pragmatism. In Colin Lankshear and Peter McLaren (Eds.) *Critical Literacy: Politics, Praxis, and the Postmodern*, pp. 217–245. Albany: State University of New York Press.

Carlson, D. (1993b, April). *Constructing the Margins: Of Multicultural Education and Curriculum Settlements.* Paper presented at the annual meeting of the American Educational Research Association, Atlanta, GA.

Carrel, P. (1987). Content and formal schemata in ESL reading. *TESOL Quarterly*, 21 (3), pp. 461–481.

Cazden, C. and Snow, C. (1990). Preface. *The Annals of the American Academy of Political and Social Science*, 508, pp. 9–11.

Cervantes, R. and Gainer, G. (1992). The effects of syntactic simplification and repetition on listening comprehension. *TESOL Quarterly*, 26 (4), pp. 767–770.

Chamot, A. and O'Malley, J. (1987). The cognitive academic language learning approach: A bridge to the mainstream. *TESOL Quarterly*, 21 (2), pp. 227–249.

Chapelle, C. and Roberts, C. (1986). Ambiguity tolerance and field independence as predictors of proficiency in English as a second language. *Language Learning*, 36, pp. 27–45.

Chomsky, N. (1965). *Aspects of the Theory of Syntax*. Cambridge: The MIT Press.

Chomsky, N. (1971). Basic principles. In J. Allen and Paul Buren (Eds.) *Chomsky: Selected Readings*, pp. 1-21. London, New York, and Toronto: Oxford University Press.

Chomsky, N. (1977). *Essays on Form and Interpretation*. New York and Amsterdam: North-Holland.

Chomsky, N. (1981). *Regras e Representações: A Inteligência Humana e seu Produto*. Rio de Janeiro: Zahar.

Chomsky, N. (1988). *Language and Problems of Knowledge: The Managua Lectures*. Cambridge: The MIT Press.

Clark, K. and Holquist, M. (1984). *Mikhail Bakhtin*. Cambridge and London: Harvard University Press.

Clark, K. and Holquist, M. (1986). A continuing dialogue. *Slavic and East European Journal*, 30 (1), pp. 96-102.

Clyne, M. (1972). *Perspectives on Language Contact*. Melbourne: Hawthorn.

Clyne, M. (1980). Typology and grammatical convergence among related languages in contact. *Review of Applied Linguistics*, 49, pp. 21–35.

Collier, V. (1987). Age and rate of acquisition of second language for academic purposes. *TESOL Quarterly*, 21 (4), pp. 617–641.

Connor, U. and Kaplan, R. (1987). *Writing Across Languages*. Reading: Addison-Wesley.

Corson, D. (1993). *Language, Minority Education and Gender: Linking Social Justice and Power*. Toronto: Ontario Institute for Studies in Education.

Crago, M. (1992). Communicative interaction and second language acquisition: An Inuit example. *TESOL Quarterly*, 26 (3), pp. 487–505.

Crookes, G. (1991). Second language speech production research. *Studies in Second Language Acquisition*, 13 (2), pp. 113–132.

Crowley, T. (1989). Bakhtin and the history of the language. In Ken Hirschkop and David Shepherd (Eds.) *Bakhtin and Cultural Theory*, pp. 68–90. Manchester and New York: Manchester University Press.

Cummins, J. (1984). *Bilingualism and Special Education: Issues in Assessment and Pedagogy*. San Diego: College Hill Press.

Cummins, J. (1986). Empowering minority students: A framework for intervention. *Harvard Educational Review*, 56 (1), pp. 372–390.

Cummins, J. (1991). Empowering minority students: A framework for intervention. In Masahiko Minami and Bruce Kennedy (Eds.) *Language Issues in Literacy and Bilingual/Multicultural Education*, pp. 372–390. Cambridge: Harvard University Press.

Cummins, J. (1993). Negotiating identities in the ESL classroom. *Contact*, 14, pp. 30–32.

Cummins, J. (in press a). Primary language instruction and the education of language minority students. In C. Leyla (Ed.) *Schooling and Language Minority Students*. Los Angeles: Evaluation and Assessment Center.

Cummins, J. (in press b). *Power and Pedagogy in the Education of Culturally Diverse Students*.

Cziko, G. (1992). The evaluation of bilingual education: From necessity and probability to possibility. *Educational Researcher*, 21 (2), pp. 10–15.

Danow, D. (1991). *The Thought of Mikhail Bakhtin: From Word to Culture*. New York: St. Martin's Press.

Darder, A. (1991). *Culture and Power in the Classroom: A Critical Foundation for Bicultural Education*. New York and London: Bergin & Garvey.

Delpit, L. (1988). The silenced dialogue: Power and pedagogy in educating other people's children. *Harvard Educational Review*, 58 (3), pp. 280–298.

Derrida, J. (1976). *Of Grammatology* (Gayatri Spivak, Trans.). Baltimore and London: Johns Hopkins University Press.

Diaz-Guerrero, R. and Szalay, L. (1991). *Understanding Mexicans and Americans: Cultural Perspectives in Conflict*. New York and London: Plenum Press.

Dorian, N. (1973). Grammatical change in a dying dialect. *Language*, 49, pp. 414–438.

Doughty, C. and Pica, T. (1986). "Information gap" tasks: Do they facilitate comprehension? *TESOL Quarterly*, 20, pp. 305–325.

Dunn, L. (1987). *Bilingual Hispanic Children on the U.S. Mainland: A Review of Research on their Cognitive, Linguistic, and Scholastic Development*. Circle Pines: American Guidance Service.

Edmonds, R. (1979). Effective schools of the urban poor. *Educational Leadership*, 37 (1), pp. 15–27.

Ellsworth, E. (1992). Why doesn't this feel empowering? Working through the repressive myths of critical pedagogy. In Carmen Luke and Jennifer Gore (Eds.) *Feminisms and Critical Pedagogy*, pp. 90–119. New York and London: Routledge.

Elsasser, N. and Steiner, V. (1987). Interactionist approach to advancing literacy. In Ira Shor (Ed.) *Freire for the Classroom: A Sourcebook for Liberatory Teaching*, pp. 45–62. Portsmouth: Boynton/Cook.

Epstein, N. (1977). *Language, Ethnicity, and the Schools: Policy Alternatives for Bilingual-Bicultural Education*. Washington, D.C.: The Institute for Educational Leadership.

Fiore, K. and Elsasser, N. (1987). Strangers no more: A liberatory literacy curriculum. In Ira Shor (Ed.) *Freire for the Classroom: A Sourcebook for Liberatory Teaching*, pp. 87–103. Portsmouth: Boynton/Cook.

Fishman, J. (1994). Interview. *BEOutreach*, Fall, pp. 26–29.

Fixman, C. (1990). The foreign language needs of U.S. based corporations. *The Annals of the American Academy of Political and Social Science*, 511, pp. 25–46.

Flege, J. and Hillenbrand, J. (1984). Limits on phonetic accuracy in foreign language production. *Journal of the Acoustical Society of America*, 76, pp. 708–721.

Foucault, M. (1972). *The Archaeology of Knowledge and the Discourse on Language*. New York: Pantheon Books.

Foucault, M. (1977). *Language, Counter-Memory, Practice: Selected Essays and Interviews*. New York: Cornell University Press.

Freire, P. (1993). *Pedagogy of the Oppressed* (Myra Bergman Ramos, Trans.). New York: Continuum.

Freire, P. and Faundez, A. (1989). *Learning to Question*. New York: Continuum.

García, O. and Otheguy, R. (1994). The value of speaking a LOTE in U.S. business. *The Annals of the American Academy of Political and Social Science*, 532, pp. 99–122.

Gardiner, M. (1992). *The Dialogics of Critique: M. M. Bakhtin and the Theory of Ideology*. London: Routledge.

Genesee, F. (1985). Second language learning through immersion: A review of U.S. programs. *Review of Educational Research*, 55 (4), pp. 541–561.

Giroux, H. (1988a). Literacy and the pedagogy of voice and political empowerment. *Educational Theory*, 38 (1), pp. 61–75.

Giroux, H. (1988b) *Schooling and the Struggle for Public Life: Critical Pedagogy in the Modern Age*. Minneapolis: University of Minnesota Press.

Glisan, E. and Drescher, V. (1993). Textbook grammar: Does it reflect native speaker speech? *The Modern Language Journal*, 77 (1), pp. 23–33.

Gore, J. (1992). *The Struggle for Pedagogies: Critical and Feminist Discourses As Regimes of Truth*. New York: Routledge.

Gramsci, A. (1988). Popular culture. In David Forgacs (Ed.) *An Antonio Gramsci Reader: Selected Writings, 1916–1935*, pp. 363–373. New York: Schocken.

Green, J. (1993). Student attitudes toward communicative and non-communicative activities: Do enjoyment and effectiveness go together? *The Modern Language Journal*, 77 (1), pp. 1–10.

Gutiérrez, F. (1985). Bicultural personality development: A process model. In Eugene Garcia and Raymond Padilla (Eds.) *Advances in Bilingual Education Research*, pp. 96–124. Tucson: The University of Arizona Press.

Hakuta, K. and Cancino, H. (1991). Trends in second-language-acquisition research. In Masahiko Minami and Bruce Kennedy (Eds.) *Language Issues in Literacy and Bilingual/Multicultural Education*, pp. 74–97. Cambridge: Harvard University Press.

Halliday, M. (1974). *The Linguistic Sciences and Language Teaching*. London: William Clowes.

Halliday, M. and Hasan, R. (1985). *Language, Context, and Text: Aspects of Language in a Social-Semiotic Perspective*. Victoria: Deakin University Press.

Harry, B. (1992). An ethnographic study of cross-cultural communication with Puerto Rican-American families in the special education system. *American Educational Research Journal*, 29 (3), pp. 471–494.

Hirschkop, K. (1989a). Critical work on the Bakhtin circle: A bibliographical essay. In Ken Hirschkop and David Shepherd (Eds.) *Bakhtin and Cultural Theory*, pp. 195–212. Manchester and New York: Manchester University Press.

Hirschkop, K. (1989b). Introduction: Bakhtin and Cultural Theory. In Ken Hirschkop and David Shepherd (Eds.) *Bakhtin and Cultural Theory*, pp. 1–38. Manchester and New York: Manchester University Press.

Hitchcock, P. (1993). *Dialogics of the Oppressed*. Minneapolis and London: University of Minnesota Press.

Holquist, M. (1990). *Dialogism: Bakhtin and His World.* London and New York: Routledge.

hooks, b. (1993). A revolution of values: The promise of multi-cultural change. *The Journal of the Midwest Modern Language Association,* 26 (1), pp. 4–11.

Hornberger, N. (1990). Bilingual education and English-only: A language-planning framework. *The Annals of the American Academy of Political and Social Science,* 508, pp. 12–26.

Humphrey, R. (1977). The effects of language dominance as determined by the Shutt Primary Language Indicator Test on the measurement of the intellectual abilities and achievement ratings of Mexican-American children in K, 1, 2 grades. Unpublished doctoral dissertation, Northern Arizona University, Arizona.

Imhoff, G. (1990). The position of U.S. English on bilingual education. *The Annals of the American Academy of Political and Social Science,* 508, pp. 48–61.

Izzo, S. (1981). *Second Language Learning: A Review of Related Studies.* Rosslyn: National Clearinghouse for Bilingual Education.

Janmohamed, A. (1994). Some implications of Paulo Freire's border pedagogy. In Henry Giroux and Peter McLaren (Eds.) *Between Borders: Pedagogy and the Politics of Cultural Studies,* pp. 242–252. New York and London: Routledge.

Kane, P. (1967, March). *The Senate Debate on the 1964 Civil Rights Act.* Doctoral dissertation, Purdue University, Ann Arbor, MI.

Kasper, G. and Dahl, M. (1991). Research methods in interlanguage pragmatics. *Studies in Second Language Acquisition,* 13 (2), pp. 215–247.

Kennedy, W. (1987). The ideological captivity of the non-poor. In Alice Evans, Robert Evans, and William Kennedy (Eds.) *Pedagogies for the Non-Poor,* pp. 232–256. New York: Maryknoll.

Kobayashi, T. (1992). Native and nonnative reactions to ESL compositions. *TESOL Quarterly,* 26 (1), pp. 81–112.

Koopmans, M. (1991). Reasoning in two languages: An assessment of the reasoning ability of Puerto Rican elementary school children. *Linguistics and Education,* 3, pp. 345–358.

Krashen, S., Long, M., and Scarcella, R. (1979). Age, rate, and eventual attainment in second language acquisition. *TESOL Quarterly,* 13, pp. 573–582.

Labov, W. (1972). *Language in the Inner City: Studies in the Black English Vernacular.* Philadelphia: University of Pennsylvania Press.

Labov, W. (1991). *Sociolinguistic Patterns.* Philadelphia: University of Pennsylvania Press.

Lambert, R. (1994). Problems and processes in U.S. foreign language planning. *The Annals of the American Academy of Political and Social Science,* 532, pp. 47–58.

Landry, R. (1974). A comparison of second language learners and monolinguals on divergent thinking tasks at the elementary level. *The Modern Language Journal,* 58, pp. 10–15.

Lessow-Hurley, J. (1991). *A Commonsense Guide to Bilingual Education.* Alexandria: ASCD.

Li, C. and Thompson, S. (1981). *Mandarin Chinese: A Functional Reference Grammar.* Berkeley: University of California Press.

Lincoln, Y. and Guba, E. (1985). *Naturalistic Inquiry.* Newbury Park: Sage.

Long, M. and Porter, P. (1985). Group work, interlanguage talk, and second language acquisition. *TESOL Quarterly,* 19, pp. 207–228.

Lucas, T., Henze, R., and Donato, R. (1990). Promoting the success of Latino language-minority students: An exploratory study of six high schools. *Harvard Educational Review,* 60 (3), pp. 315–340.

Luft, C. (1985). *Língua e liberdade: Por uma nova concepção da língua materna.* Porto Alegre: L & PM.

Luke, C. and Gore, J. (Eds.) (1992). *Feminisms and Critical Pedagogy.* New York and London: Routledge.

Lyons, J. (1990). The past and future directions of federal bilingual-education policy. *The Annals of the American Academy of Political and Social Science,* 508, pp. 66–80.

Macedo, D. (1993). Literacy for stupidification: The pedagogy of big lies. *Harvard Educational Review,* 63 (2), pp. 183–206.

Madrid, A. (1990). Official English: A false policy issue. *The Annals of the American Academy of Political and Social Science,* 508, pp. 62–65.

Madrid, D. and Garcia, E. (1985). The effect of language transfer on bilingual proficiency. In Eugene Garcia and Raymond Padilla (Eds.) *Advances in Bilingual Education Research,* pp. 53–70. Tucson: The University of Arizona Press.

Malcuzynski, P. (1990). Mikhail Bakhtin and the sociocritical practice. *Discours Social/Social Discourse,* 3 (1 and 2), pp. 81–97.

Man, P. (1989). Dialogue and dialogism. In Gary Morson and Caryl Emerson (Eds.) *Rethinking Bakhtin: Extensions and Challenges*, pp. 105–114. Evanston: Northwestern University Press.

Marger, M. (1994). *Race and Ethnic Relations: American and Global Perspectives*. Belmont: Wadsworth.

McClellan, W. (1990). The dialogic other: Bakhtin's theory of rhetoric. *Discours Social/Social Discourse*, 3 (1 and 2), pp. 233–249.

McGroarty, M. (1992). The societal context of bilingual education. *Educational Researcher*, 21 (2), pp. 7–9.

McIntosh, P. (1989). White privilege: Unpacking the invisible knapsack. *Peace and Freedom*, July/August, pp. 10–12.

McLaren, P. (1989). *Life in Schools: An Introduction to Critical Pedagogy in the Foundations of Education*. New York and London: Longman.

McLaren, P. (1993a). Critical literacy and postcolonial praxis: A Freirean perspective. *College Literature*, 20 (1), pp. 7–27.

McLaren, P. (1993b). White terror and oppositional agency: Towards a critical multiculturalism. *Strategies*, 7, pp. 98–131.

McLaren, P. (1993c). An interview with Marcia Moraes of Brazil: Brazil—myth and reality. *International Journal of Educational Reform*, 2 (3), pp. 309–315.

McLaren, P. (1994a). *Life in Schools: An Introduction to Critical Pedagogy in the Foundations of Education*. New York and London: Longman.

McLaren, P. (1994b). An exchange with Eugene E. Garcia, Director of the Office of Bilingual Education and Minority Language Affairs, U.S. Department of Education. *International Journal of Educational Reform*, 3 (1), pp. 74–80.

McLaren, P. (1994c). Postmodernism and the death of politics: A Brazilian reprieve. In Peter McLaren and Colin Lankshear (Eds.) *Politics of Liberation: Paths from Freire*, pp. 193–215. London and New York: Routledge.

McLaren, P. (1995). *Critical Pedagogy and Predatory Culture: Oppositional Politics in a Postmodern Era*. London and New York: Routledge.

McLaren, P. and Lankshear, C. (1993). Critical literacy and the postmodern turn. In Colin Lankshear and Peter McLaren (Eds.) *Critical Literacy: Politics, Praxis, and the Postmodern*, pp. 379–419. Albany, N.Y.: State University of New York Press.

McLaren, P. and Lankshear, C. (Eds.) (1994). *Politics of Liberation: Paths from Freire*. London and New York: Routledge.

McLaren, P. and Leonard, P. (Eds.) (1993). *Paulo Freire: A Critical Encounter.* London and New York: Routledge.

Medvedev, P. (1978). *The Formal Method in Literary Scholarship: A Critical Introduction to Sociological Poetics* (Albert Wehrle, Trans.). Baltimore and London: Johns Hopkins University Press.

Moll, L. (1992). Bilingual classroom studies and community analysis: Some recent trends. *Educational Researcher,* 21 (2), pp. 20–24.

Moore, S. (1994). Intervention strategies in foreign language planning. *The Annals of The American Academy of Political and Social Science,* 532, pp. 74–87.

Moraes, M. (1992a, April). *Linguistic performance and schooling.* Paper presented at the annual meeting of the American Educational Research Association, San Francisco, CA.

Moraes, M. (1992b). Review of *Paulo Freire: A Critical Encounter. Journal of Education,* 174 (3), pp. 128–135.

Morson, G. (1986). The Baxtin industry. *Slavic and East European Journal,* 30 (1), pp. 81–90.

Morson, G. and Emerson, C. (1989). Introduction: Rethinking Bakhtin. In Gary Morson and Caryl Emerson (Eds.) *Rethinking Bakhtin: Extensions and Challenges,* pp. 1–60. Evanston: Northwestern University Press.

Nava, C. (1993, August). *The practice of patriotism: Official versions of national identity in the Brazilian public school, 1937–1975.* Paper presented at the annual meeting of the American Historical Association, Pacific Coast Branch.

Nieto, S. (1992). *Affirming Diversity.* New York: Longman.

Nieto, S. (1993). Linguistic diversity in multicultural classrooms. In H. Svi Shapiro & David E. Purpel (Eds.) *Critical Social Issues in American Education: Toward the 21st Century,* pp. 194–211. New York and London: Longman.

Nunan, D. (1987). Does instruction make a difference? Revisited. *TESOL Quarterly,* 21 (2), pp. 372–377.

Nunan, D. (1991). Methods in second language classroom-oriented research. *Studies in Second Language Acquisition,* 13 (2), pp. 249–269.

O'Connor, T. and Quantz, R. (1991). Critical pedagogy, cultural politics, and professional education. In John Hancock and William Miller (Eds. ) *Architecture: Back . . . to . . . life,* pp. 277–281. Proceedings of the 79th Annual Meeting of the Association of Collegiate Schools of Architecture: ACSA Press.

Oh, J. (1992). The effects of L2 reading assessment methods on anxiety level. *TESOL Quarterly*, 26 (1), pp. 172–176.

Oldenski, T. (1994). Liberation theology and critical pedagogy: Theory and practice at an alternative school site. Unpublished doctoral dissertation. Miami University, Oxford, Ohio.

Otheguy, R. (1991). Thinking about bilingual education: A critical appraisal. In Masahiko and Bruce Kennedy (Eds.) *Language Issues in Literacy and Bilingual/Multicultural Education*, pp. 409–423. Cambridge: Harvard University Press.

Pedraza, P. and Attinasi, J. (1980, June). Rethinking diglossia. Paper presented at the conference Ethnoperspectives in Bilingual Education Research, Eastern Michigan University, MI.

Perini, M. (1986). *Para uma Nova Gramática do Português*. São Paulo: Ática.

Peters, M. and Lankshear, C. (1994). Education and hermeneutics: A Freirean interpretation. In Peter McLaren and Colin Lankshear (Eds.) *Politics of Liberation: Paths from Freire*, pp. 173–192. London and New York: Routledge.

Phillips, E. (1992). The effects of language anxiety on students' oral test performance and attitudes. *The Modern Language Journal*, 76 (1), pp. 14–26.

Ponzio, A. (1990). Bakhtinian alterity and the search for identity in Europe today. *Discours Social/Social Discourse*, 3 (1 and 2), pp. 217–227.

Quantz, R. and O'Connor, T. (1988). Writing critical ethnography: Dialogue, multivoicedness, and carnival in cultural texts. *Educational Theory*, 38 (1), pp. 95–109.

Ramirez, D. (1991). Study finds native language instruction is a plus. *NABE NEWS*, 14 (5), pp. 19–21.

Reyes, M. (1992). Challenging venerable assumptions: Literacy instruction for linguistically different students. *Harvard Educational Review*, 62 (4), pp. 427–444.

Roller, C. and Matambo, A. (1992). Bilingual readers' use of background knowledge in learning from text. *TESOL Quarterly*, 26 (1), pp. 129–141.

Rosenthal, A., Baker, K., and Ginsburg, A. (1983). The effect of language background on achievement level and learning among elementary school students. *Sociology of Education*, 56, pp. 157–169.

San Miguel Jr., G. (1987). The status of historical research on Chicano education. *Review of Educational Research*, 57 (4), pp. 467–480.

Saussure, F. (1959). *Course in General Linguistics* (W. Baskin, Trans.). New York: McGraw-Hill.

Scott, J. (1992). Multiculturalism and the politics of identity. *October*, 61, pp. 12–19.

Scott, M. (1986). Student affective reactions to oral language tests. *Language Testing*, 3, pp. 99–118.

Secada, W. (1990). Research, politics, and bilingual education. *The Annals of the American Academy of Political and Social Science*, 508, pp. 62–65.

Segalowitz, N. (1977). Psychological perspectives on bilingual education. In B. Spolsky and R. Cooper (Eds.) *Frontier of Bilingual Education*, pp. 45–62. Rowley: Newbury House.

Shor, I. and Freire, P. (1987). *A Pedagogy for Liberation: Dialogues on Transforming Education*. Massachusetts: Bergin & Garvey.

Silva, T. and McLaren, P. (1993). Knowledge under siege: The Brazilian debate. In Peter McLaren and Peter Leonard (Eds.) *Paulo Freire: A Critical Encounter*, pp. 36–46. London and New York: Routledge.

Sleeter, C. and Grant, C. (1988). *Making Choices for Multicultural Education: Five Approaches to Race, Class, and Gender*. Columbus, Toronto, and London: Merril Publishing Company.

So, A. and Chan, K. (1984). What matters? The relative impact of language background and socioeconomic status on reading achievement. *The Journal of National Association for Bilingual Education*, 8, pp. 27–41.

Stam, R. (1989). Mikhail Bakhtin and left cultural critique. In E. Ann Kaplan (Ed.) *Postmodernism and Its Discontents*, pp. 116–145. London and New York: Verso.

Starr, F. (1994). Foreign language on the campus: Room for improvement. *The Annals of The American Academy of Political and Social Science*, 532, pp. 138–148.

Stein, C. (1986). *Sink or Swim: The Politics of Bilingual Education*. New York, Connecticut, and London: Praeger.

Steinberg, S. (1992). Critical multiculturalism and democratic schooling: An interview with Peter McLaren and Joe Kincheloe. *International Journal of Educational Reform*, 1 (4), pp. 392–405.

Stemmler, A. (1966). An experimental approach to the teaching of oral language and reading. *Harvard Educational Review*, 36 (1), pp. 42–59.

Stewart, D. (1993). *Immigration and Education: The Crisis and the Opportunities*. New York and Toronto: Lexington.

Stewart, S. (1986). Shouts on the street: Bakhtin's anti-linguistics. In Gary Morson (Ed.) *Bakhtin: Essays and Dialogues on His Work*, pp. 41–57. Chicago and London: University of Chicago Press.

Stoddart, J. (1854). *The Philosphy of Language; Comprehending Universal Grammar or the Pure Science of Language*. London and Glasgow: Richard Griffin.

Terdiman, R. (1985). Deconstructing memory: On representing the past and theorizing culture in France since the revolution. *Diacritics*, Winter, pp. 13–36.

Titunik, I. (1973). The formal method and the sociological method (M. M. Baxtin, P. N. Medvedev, V. N. Volosinov) in Russian theory and study of literature. In V. N. Volosinov *Marxism and the Philosophy of Language*, pp. 175–200. New York and London: Seminar Press.

Titunik, I. (1986). The Baxtin problem: Concerning Katerina Clark and Michael Holquist's Mikhail Bakhtin. *Slavic and East European Journal*, 30 (1), pp. 91–95.

Torres, C. and Freire, P. (1994). Twenty years after *Pedagogy of the Oppressed*: Paulo Freire in conversation with Carlos Alberto Torres. In Peter McLaren and Colin Lankshear (Eds.) *Politics of Liberation: Paths from Freire*, pp. 100–107. London and New York: Routledge.

Tyndall, B. (1991). What influences raters' judgment of student writing. *Linguistics and Education*, 3, pp. 191–202.

U.S. Congressional Record (1964), *88th Congress, 2nd Session*, Vol. 110.

Vanpatten, B. and Cadierno, T. (1993). Input processing and second language acquisition: A role for instruction. *The Modern Language Journal*, 77 (1), pp. 45–57.

Voloshinov, V. (1973). *Marxism and the Philosophy of Language* (L. Matejka and I. R. Titunik, Trans.). New York and London: Seminar Press.

Voloshinov, V. (1976). *Freudianism: A Marxist Critique* (I. R.Titunik, Trans.). New York, San Francisco, and London: Academic Press.

Vygotsky, L. (1978). *Mind in Society: The Development of Higher Psychological Process.* (M. Cole, V. Steiner, S. Scribner, and E. Soubermor, Trans.). Massachusetts and London: Harvard University Press.

Walsh, C. (1991). *Pedagogy and the Struggle for Voice: Issues of Language, Power, and Schooling for Puerto Ricans.* New York and London: Bergin & Garvey.

Wehrle, A. (1978). Introduction: M. M. Bakhtin/P. N. Medvedev. In P. N. Medvedev/M. M. Bakhtin *The Formal Method in Literary Scholarship: A Critical Introduction to Sociological Poetics* (Albert Wehrle, Trans.), pp. ix–xxiii. Baltimore and London: Johns Hopkins University Press.

Weiler, K. (1994). Freire and a feminist pedagogy of difference. In Peter McLaren and Colin Lankshear (Eds.) *Politics of Liberation: Paths from Freire* (pp. 12–40). London and New York: Routledge.

Wertsch, J. (1985). *Vygotsky and the Social Formation of Mind.* Cambridge and London: Harvard University Press.

Willig, A. (1985). A meta-analysis of selected studies on the effectiveness of bilingual education. *Review of Educational Research,* 55 (3), pp. 269–317.

Winant, H. (1992). The other side of the process: Racial formation in contemporary Brazil. In George Yúdice, Jean Franco, and Juan Flores (Eds.) *On Edge: The Crisis of Contemporary Latin American Culture,* pp. 85–113. Minneapolis and London: University of Minnesota Press.

Young, D. (1991). The relationship between anxiety and foreign language oral proficiency ratings. In Elaine Horwitz and Dolly Young (Eds.) *Language Anxiety: From Theory and Research to Classroom Implications,* pp. 23–42. Englewood Cliffs: Prentice-Hall.

# AUTHOR INDEX

Abella, Rodolfo, 86
Abraham, R., 86
Ada, Alma, 123, 125
Ambert, Alba, 43
Attinasi, John, 69
August, Diane, 45, 59

Back, Eurico, 79
Baker, Keith, 45, 48, 53, 86
Bakhtin, Mikhail, 1, 7, 9–11, 13–15, 35, 95, 96, 119; and connection to Marxism, 16; and consciousness, 70, 101; and dialogized context, 127; disputed texts of, 16, 19; and heteroglossia, 23, 135; and language, 85, 94, 134; life of, 13; and linguistic relationships, 23; and otherness, 25; and sign, 20; and stratification of language, 21, 22; and understanding, 29, 32, 77, 78, 131; and utterance, 26, 27, 29; and word, 21, 94
Bally, Charles, 33
Barnes, Robert, 42
Bhabha, Homi, xi, xii
*Bilingual Hispanic Children on the U. S. Mainland: A Review of Research on their Cognitive, Linguistic, and Scholastic Development* (Dunn), 130n. 1
*Boston Globe*, 50, 51

Cadierno, T., 84
Cancino, Herlinda, 70–73

Caramazza, Alfonso, 68
Carbone, E., 68
Cardenas, Jose, 55
Carlson, Dennis, 9, 137
Carrel, Patricia, 85
Cazden, Courtney, 41, 42, 64
Cervantes, Raoul, 85
Chamot, Anna, 86
Chan, Kenyon, 86
Chapelle, Carol, 86
Chomsky, Noam, 1, 7, 8, 10, 32, 71, 79, 80, 122
Clark, Katerina, 14–19
Clyne, M., 68
Collier, Virginia, 86
*Condition of Bilingual Education in The Nation: A Report to The Congress and The President, The* (U.S. Department of Education), 59
Connor, Ulla, 71
Corson, David, 66
*Course in General Linguistics* (Saussure), 33
Crago, Martha, 83, 84
Crookes, Graham, 85
Crowley, Tony, 95
Cummins, Jim, 2, 8, 122, 123, 126, 130, 137
Cziko, Gary, 41, 54

Dahl, Merete, 72
Danow, David, 92

153

# SUBJECT INDEX

abstract objectivism, 8; and consciousness, 29; and error analysis, 71; and language, 34–37, 77, 79, 80, 92, 122; and linguistic sign, 36, 37, 91; and universal grammar, 33, 34. *See also* sign
American Council on the Teaching of Foreign Languages, 64
Arizona, Constitution of, 48, 49
awareness: movements of social, 135. *See also* consciousness; heteroglossia

Bakhtin Circle, the: and dialogic existence, 112, 114; disputed texts of, 7, 15–19; and identity, 131, 132; and Marxian theory, 14, 19; members of, 7, 14, 15; and multivoicedness of society, 113, 114, 124; and Paulo Freire's theory, 103–106, 135; and postmodern theories, 99, 100. *See also* abstract objectivism; Bilingual Education; dialogue; sign
Bilingual Education: Act, 53–61; and the American Institute of Research, 54; bibliographic entries of, 41; in Canada, 68; and collective social awareness, 128; and contributions of the Bakhtin Circle, 89, 123, 127; and curriculum, 131; and the debate between English-plus versus English-only, 61–65; and educational decision making, 126; existing programs of, 10, 43, 44, 67–70, 136; meanings of, 42, 131, 132, 136; multicultural view of, 103, 136,137; and relevance of social

contexts, 121, 132; standard research in, 84; "successful" programs of, 120, 121; and teachers, 122, 123, 125, 126; and U. S. government, 54–59, 62
Brazil: education in, 2, 5, 6; and ethnic groups, 6; and military dictatorship, 3, 4; and Paulo Freire, 5; population of, 2

Civil Rights Act, 45–48
communication, 30, 32; main characteristic of, 31; and cultural identity, 84; and verbal intercourse, 30. *See also* language
consciousness: and Bakhtinian theory, 104; construction of, 23, 70; and ideological phenomena, 25, 101, 102; and Marxian analysis of ideology, 24, 39, 132; of the oppressive group, 114–116; and Paulo Freire's theory, 104, 105; as a process, 74, 102; and purposiveness, 101, 102; reflexive, 135; and social interaction, 26, 90, 101, 134; and social struggle, 105; speaking, 40, 69, 70, 122; and unconsciousness, 24; Vygotsky's theory of, 104, 104n.3

dialogic-linguistics, 93
dialogue: Bakhtinian sense of, 10, 94, 97, 101, 104, 106, 112, 134; and divergent social contexts, 116, 117; Freirean sense of, 104, 105, 134. *See also* Pedagogy, Dialogic